CANNERY ROW

The History of John Steinbeck's Old Ocean View Avenue
and Its Connections to the Pacific Northwest

By Michael Kenneth Hemp

With Photographs from the
Pat Hathaway Collection of California Views

Published by
The History Company
P.O. Box 31
Wauna (Gig Harbor), WA 98395
www.TheHistoryCompany.com

THE HISTORY COMPANY

P.O. Box 31
Wauna (Gig Harbor), WA, USA
www.thehistorycompany.com
mkhemp@thehistorycompany.com
(831) 236-2990

Fifth Edition: March, 2022.

LIBRARY OF CONGRESS CATALOGING-IN-PUBLICATION DATA

Hemp, Michael Kenneth, 1942-
    Cannery Row: the history of old ocean view avenue and its
            connections to the pacific northwest
    Bibliography: p.
    Includes index.
    1. Cannery Row (Monterey, Calif.) 2. Monterey (Calif.)-History
    3. Steinbeck, John, 1902-1968-Homes and haunts-California-Monterey
I. Title
F869.M7H35 1986   979.4'76   86-32023

Fifth Edition, First Printing
        ISBN 13: 978-0-941425-06-3

Publication design by Bridges Design Group, Los Angeles

Printed in the USA

Primary photography in this book is available from
THE PAT HATHAWAY HISTORICAL PHOTO COLLECTION OF CALIFORNIA VIEWS

www.caviews.com

IN MEMORIAM

*Pat Hathaway, my closest colleague for 4 decades of shared Cannery Row, Ed Ricketts, and John Steinbeck
research and publication passed away unexpectedly in January 2021 of myasthenia gravis (an agent orange related disease).
He will be missed by generations inspired by his kindness and knowledge, as well as his passion for the archival photographic
collection bearing his name that has touched untold legions of souls with the accurate visions and understanding of our past,
and what it should mean to our future.*

His spectacular collection will live on at the Monterey County Historical Society Museum, Salinas, California.

Pat Hathaway at the Lab.   Michael Hemp [2009-007-001]

There are over 80,000 images in the Pat Hathaway Photo Collection of California Views historical photo archive including Monterey, Cannery Row, Carmel, Pacific Grove, Pebble Beach, Carmel Valley, Point Lobos, Big Sur, Salinas, the San Francisco earthquake and fire, all of the California Missions, and photography of Ed Ricketts in Monterey, Mexico, and the Pacific Northwest. Please see our web site for a more complete listing.

The Pat Hathaway Collection catalog numbers are indicated in brackets under each photo. Inquiries for photo reproductions or enlargements should be accompanied by the catalog number and a brief description of the subject and page number in this book. Please specify the Edition and which Printing, as they now vary over the decades this book has been in print since 1986.

DEDICATION

THIS BOOK IS DEDICATED TO THE CANNERY ROW "ALUMNI"— THE MEN AND WOMEN WHO WORKED ITS CANNERIES AND THE MEN WHO BRAVED THE PACIFIC FOR ITS SILVER HARVEST.

Cannery Row district, Monterey, California, 1945.   *[Fairchild photo]*

EXPANDED FIFTH EDITION

Each successive edition of this book on Cannery Row's history since 1986 has been updated, refined and improved. The exclusive photography from the Pat Hathaway Collection of California Views has been refined by digital imaging improvement and, in many cases, the photographic images have been re-scanned from original negatives or photographs. We have endeavored to identify and display photographer's credits insofar as possible.

The special PART TWO section of this Expanded Edition contains research in progress and representations are subject to new or additional data, information, or credits as may become available–and will be clarified or corrected in subsequent printings of the Fifth and subsequent editions of this book.

For up to date information and materials on historic Cannery Row, go to:

www.TheHistoryCompany.com

www.caviews.com

www.CanneryRow.org

www.SardineKing.com

www.WesternFlyer.org

www.CanneryRow.net

www.mchsmuseum.com

www.monterey.org

Cover Photo: George Seideneck [72-012-053]
Cannery Row's enclosed conveyor cross-overs, 1945, with cannery worker, Hank Damewood.

SPECIAL THANKS

My Special Thanks go to the following people, without whom this book would not have been possible:

Charles Nonella, Frank Wright, Pat Hathaway, Horace "Sparky" Enea, Skipper Tony Berry, Tom Mangelsdorf, William B. Brown, Edward Ricketts, Jr., Fred Strong, Joanna Livesay, Thom Steinbeck, Jackson Benson, Will Shaw and the The Thomas Doud Sr. and Anita M. Doud Fund of the Community Foundation for Monterey County, The Cannery Row Foundation, Skipper Salvatore Enea, Skipper Horace Balbo, Betty Hoag McGlynn, Mrs. Wesley Dodge, Skipper James Davi, Frank and Grace Bergara, Al and Esther Campoy, Dorothy Wheeler, Beth Robinson, Eldon Dedini, Tom Weber, Antonette Villines, Ray "Spats" Lucido, Robert V. Enea, Ted Melicia, Frank Tanaka, John Gota, Seizo Kodani, Francisco "Paco" Ferro, Maury Cooper, Bernard Jaksha, Frank Crispo, Daryl Stokes, John Stidham, Kalisa Moore, Dick O'kane, Michael Maiorana, Anna Nowak and the Paquin Family, Anne-Marie Colendich, David Hemp, Sally Hanhy, Robert Edison, Bob Lippi, Herb and Robbie Behrens, Neal and Bettina Hotelling, Bill Johnk, Dennis Copeland, Sandy Lydon, Tim Thomas, Jake Stock, Mike Marotta, Katharine Rodger, Eric Enno Tamm, Larry Tsuneo Oda, Steve Eddy, James Bridges, Ted Balestreri, Abel Quinones, Gerry Low-Sabado, Tom and Margie Morjig...and all the colleagues, cannery workers, skippers and fishermen, laborers and residents of the Old Row who have assisted in the nearly four decades of this research.

I owe very special thanks to my wife, Terri Adrienne Wolfson, for her tireless support, patience and perseverance as an innocent casualty of my historical and artistic crucible.

PART TWO

New Horizons for Cannery Row-Monterey and Pacific Northwest History

SPECIAL THANKS

Jerry Elfendahl, Michael Fredson, Nancy Ricketts, Pat Hathaway, Ed Ricketts Jr., Kevin Bailey, Ole Anderson, Jan Parker, Shirley Erhart, Colin Levings, Dennis and Yvonne Fry, John Gregg, Wesley Wenhardt, Ron Karabaich, Allen Petrich, Ole Knudson, Richard Astro, Don Kohrs, Gregor and Di Cailliet, Bill Baarsma, Dale Wirsing, Tracy Rebsock, Eric Enno Tamm, Kenneth and Marlene Mack, Clare Petrich, James and Aimee Wu, Nancy Starr, James Bridges, Chris Chase, Peter Hemp, Brendan Baalam, Lowell Anderson, Judy Romeo, Vicky Glasetter, Beverly Hooley (Tex Travis daughter), Steve Hooley, Gilbert Travis, Gerry (Berry) Schwartz, Dan Schwartz, Dan Schwartz Jr., Kathy Buzzard, Larry Buzzard, Nick Mullan, Linda Pitcher, Jamison Murphy, James Perry, Caroline and Bob Burreson, Laura Barber, Doug Johnson, David Larson, Dave Demick, Dave Bayley, and the many researched family members, community, museum staff, and archivists that have supported this work.

CHARLIE NONELLA

In 1983, Charlie Nonella stepped out of the crowd at the Great Cannery Row Reunion and said, "You should talk to me." We talked almost daily for the next four years. Charlie Nonella had not only been a cannery worker with a bad reputation on old Ocean View Avenue, but he also happened to be the best friend and constant companion of another cannery worker, Harold Otis Bicknell, otherwise known in the canneries and around Monterey by his nickname, "Gabe."

John Steinbeck wrote to his editor at Viking Press, Pat Covici, that Gabe was his model for Mack, of "Mack and the boys" in his 1945 Cannery Row. Gabe was, indeed, the leader of an alcoholic group of roughnecks on Cannery Row that lived and drank and often worked together in the sardine factories of the Old Row. They lived in about every flophouse in the Cannery Row district—including one called the Palace, above the tracks behind Flora's "Lone Star Cafe."

Charlie claimed to be the best "can catcher" on the Row at filling cases with sardine cans fed from a chute in the warehouse at Hovden's. I heard his claim grudgingly confirmed by others who also vouched for his well-earned reputation for drinking and fighting. His pal, Gabe Bicknell, was the kind of mechanic that machines just seemed to run better around.

Gabe (Mack in "Cannery Row") could fix anything, a valuable talent in the canneries of Ocean View Avenue which were often maintained with a minimum of investment. Gabe and Charlie had an interesting operating plan. They never worked for a cannery a few days and then got drunk and fired. They worked for weeks, sometime months at a time, before allowing their drinking to cost them their jobs. When they went back looking for work, as proven, highly qualified, hard working cannery laborers, they got hired again.

Charlie was in a sanitarium with tuberculosis when Gabe died in a house fire in 1954. He stopped drinking "cold turkey" in 1960 and saved his sight and his life. He smoked like a chimney and was never without a thermos of horrid black coffee. But his mind was like a camera. He accurately recalled details of his years on the Row: names, dates, people, events, work in the canneries. He was even a bouncer in one of the Row's whorehouses. Charlie Nonella shot a string of continuity, perspective and accuracy through my research I could never have achieved without him.

Charlie, like Gabe, was an accomplished specimen collector for Ed Ricketts and made several, rather routine, frog collecting trips to Carmel Valley, as reported in Cannery Row. I still miss him and thank him often for sharing his invaluable knowledge and memories of his life on Ocean View Avenue. He and Pat Hathaway made this book possible.

Ray Santella photo

Charlie Nonella receiving the Cannery Row Foundation's award for Cannery Worker of the Year at the Great Cannery Row Reunion of 1984. The award, presented by Michael Hemp, is a plank from the San Xavier Packing Co. (its cross-over sign in the background), a cork float from a purse-seine net, and a spike from the Southern Pacific Rail Road tracks pulled up on Cannery Row in 1984.

AUTHOR'S NOTES

Two of Cannery Row's most notable personalities have inspired the concept and design of this book: John Steinbeck and his close friend and mentor, Edward F. Ricketts. John Steinbeck's Cannery Row is a concise and easily read account of life on old Ocean View Avenue in the late 1930s, focusing on the adventures of his friend "Doc" (Ed Ricketts) and the misadventures of one of the most colorful casts of characters in American literature. John's interest and concern for the human touch in his fiction left little room, however, for facts that did not serve his nostalgic imagery.

Marine biologist Ed Ricketts loved "true things" and in the 1920s and 1930s he pursued his controversial approach to the study of marine biology with an awareness of how important context is in the discovery, explanation and understanding of physical, biological phenomena. His pioneering study of the inter-relationship of the organisms in the tide pools of the inter-tidal zone, the specialty at which he became a pioneering expert, provided the model for approaching all subjects. His Between Pacific Tides, published in 1940 by Stanford University Press, established him as the ecological leader in modern biological science.

CANNERY ROW The History of John Steinbeck's Old Ocean View Avenue is therefore concise, human and graphic, as John would like it. It is also as precise as current available research can make it. Its scope is intentionally broad enough to include the context of Monterey history necessary for an understanding and appreciation of the time and place the world has come to know as Cannery Row. I think that Ed Ricketts would further appreciate its utility in that this book—with its photography from the Pat Hathaway Historical Photo Collection and the detailed map-guide to old Ocean View Avenue—will prove especially useful to those with the opportunity to seek Cannery Row's history and the romantic nostalgia of its Steinbeck legacy in person.

Cannery Row would certainly have an historical identity of its own earned on the dubious merits of the ecological and economic disaster resulting from the collapse of the sardine fishery and the major Monterey industry it supported. It is also unfortunate that Cannery Row's unlearned ecological-economic lesson still haunts the world's oceans and collapsing fisheries today. But the men and women of the 1930s and 1940s that became subjects of John Steinbeck's Cannery Row have provided a nostalgic focal point for the whole of Monterey's canning history. The literary success of Cannery Row has elevated the street to world fame through John's wry and compassionate accounts of it, drawn largely from direct observation and participation in the decade of the thirties.

A primary objective of this book is to provide a vision of The Row as it was, from which unfolds both its emerging but little known "human history" and a vivid background for John Steinbeck's fiction. The map-guide and its indexed historical and Steinbeck landmarks serves to prepare or supplement the reading of the following books relating to Cannery Row by John Steinbeck:

Cannery Row, 1945
Sweet Thursday, the sequel to Cannery Row, 1954
Log From the Sea of Cortez, 1951 – containing the "About Ed Ricketts" preface to the restructured 1941 publication of Sea of Cortez, co-authored by John Steinbeck and Edward F. Ricketts.

With or without such preparation, however, this presentation of Monterey's fishing and canning history provides a vivid perspective designed to enhance your appreciation and enjoyment of Cannery Row, particularly as less and less remains of the Old Row. With this book and the magic of your imagination you are invited to adventure into Cannery Row. It will never be again as it was, but the future will somehow always hold its ghost.

—MICHAEL HEMP

ABOUT THE PHOTOGRAPHY

The photographs in this Fifth Edition, in all but a few instances, are now scans from original negatives and prints from the Pat Hathaway Collection of California Views. The dramatically improved photographic clarity is again augmented further by an advanced, state of the art, imaging and printing process employed in the publication of this book. Every loving effort has been made to make it, once again, an exceptionally visual history of a truly exceptional place and time.

It is important to note that photos selected for this book have been used as close to full-frame whenever possible, with cropping kept to a minimum. Due to the age and condition of some photos, variation in their clarity and contrast is unavoidable. Digital restoration has been employed extensively to preserve the integrity of the original images. In some cases, photos chosen for this publication are not only the best available, but the only images available.

TABLE OF CONTENTS

PART TWO

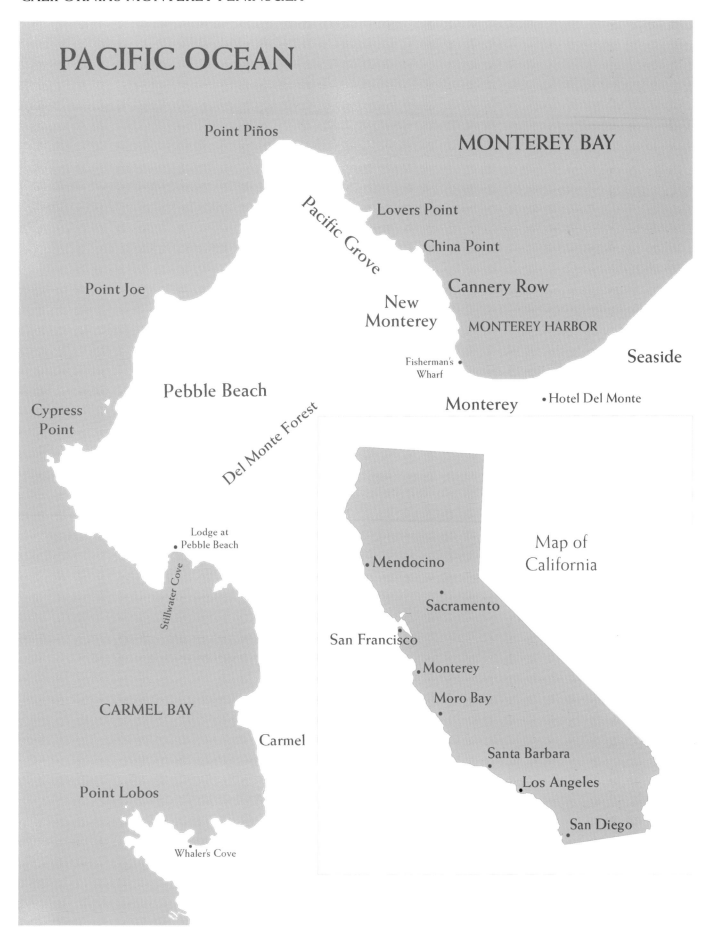

PACIFIC OCEAN

Point Piños

MONTEREY BAY

Lovers Point

China Point

Pacific Grove

Point Joe

Cannery Row

New
Monterey

MONTEREY HARBOR

Fisherman's
Wharf

Seaside

Pebble Beach

Monterey

Hotel Del Monte

Del Monte Forest

Cypress
Point

Map of
California

Lodge at
Pebble Beach

Mendocino

Sacramento

Stillwater Cove

San Francisco

Monterey

CARMEL BAY

Moro Bay

Carmel

Santa Barbara

Los Angeles

Point Lobos

San Diego

Whaler's Cove

Booth's early development of sardine packing depended on innovative and inventive personnel, many of whom went on to own or operate other canneries — all of which were forced to locate away from the harbor, along a rocky stretch of coastline out toward the Chinatown near Pacific Grove.

C. W. J. Johnson circa 1887 [GL 96-050-006]

The vacant coast south of Monterey on a road that would first host a solitary, elegant estate on this beach—which was eventually engulfed by a canyon of tin and timber sardine factories in the growth of the canning industry. Monterey's early wharf can be seen at the far left of this photo.   I. W. Taber [83-003-001]

INTRODUCTION

Cannery Row's origins are a mixture of the rocky Monterey coastline and the toil and industry of the Orient. A Chinese fishing village, from which "China Point" derives its name, was established in the early 1850s and was devastated by fire in 1906.

Monterey's first major canning operation had begun next to Fisherman's Wharf when Booth's sardine canning experiment was matched with the skill of Sicilian fishermen and "lampara" fishing techniques. Booth's early development of sardine packing depended on innovative and inventive personnel, many of whom went on to own or operate other canneries — all of which were forced to locate away from the harbor, along a rocky stretch of coastline out toward the Chinatown near Pacific Grove.

The rutty, unpaved coastal road from Monterey to Pacific Grove grew to host the sardine factories that for half a century would dominate Monterey history and commerce. In 1902, Japanese venture pioneer Otosaburo Noda and Harry Malpas of San Francisco founded the first canning operation on Ocean View Avenue. In 1958 the street was re-named "Cannery Row" in honor of a writer who few regarded very seriously when he had frequented it: John Steinbeck.

The intervening years are an epic tale of the lives, labor and fortunes at stake on Ocean View Avenue in the plunder of a seemingly inexhaustible natural resource — sardines.

Two World Wars, Prohibition and the Great Depression imprinted their marks on this famous street and its "Alumni." Fate's greatest imprint was cast with the disappearance of the sardines in the late 1940s. Depletion of the fishery, currents and pollution in the food chain have all been blamed for the demise of this once major industry and the street that supported it.

Edward F. Ricketts' famous comment, "They're all in cans" is an admitted oversimplification. Of course, he and other authorities on the fishery knew only too well the other answer,

with roots even deeper in the canning process: two thirds of Monterey's sardines never made it into cans at all. They left town on the Southern Pacific rails as 100 lb. sacks of fish meal and as sardine oil. The reduction process, which turned the silver tide into sardine by-products, was far more profitable than canning for consumption, which required a much larger labor force and sold in far less profitable markets, usually overseas against nationally subsidized industries.

Reduction profits were so attractive to the industry that in the mid-to-late 1930s they were willing to cooperate in a scheme to fit a fleet of ships converted from carrying cargo to the production of fish meal—without any limitations whatsoever, beyond the off-shore legal limits of control. Before this practice could be stopped, the ultimate damage had already been done. This is perhaps the least understood, yet most important single act in the chain of events and bad decisions that caused the near destruction of one of the globe's most incredible natural resources.

By the end of the forties, decades of warnings and urgent appeals for conservation had been ignored, ridiculed and discredited. Wartime patriotic fervor had also done little to encourage either conservation or attention to what scientists like Ed Ricketts knew only too well: Cannery Row was about to commit suicide.

The sardines virtually vanished by the early fifties. The last sardine catch was packed in 1964, with the last operating cannery, the Hovden Food Products Corporation — now the Monterey Bay Aquarium — closing its doors forever in 1973, canning squid.

The ecological disaster was, of course, mirrored by pain and human suffering as Monterey's major commercial resource mysteriously disappeared, leaving the once thriving fishing and canning industry to die on its waterfront in a ghostly gray demise. There was a time, however, when the inhabitants of this coast were far less vulnerable and dependent on the commercial bounty from the sea. And that is where this story of Cannery Row really begins...

14

FIRST INHABITANTS

It may have been the place the tribes called "Tamokt," the grassy hill overlooking the rocky hook at the south end of the long beach. To the north was the slough country, now known as Elkhorn, which provided fish, waterfowl and game for their diet, as its river wandered in wide marshes to the sea. These gentle, primitive natives were scattered in small groups along the shore and throughout the coastal and inland valleys. Their nomadic food-gathering and hunting took them wherever the seasonal foraging, game and weather provided them refuge and provision.

It is likely that from this spot the Indians witnessed Portuguese navigator Captain Juan Cabrillo's passing in November 1542, unable to anchor due to a severe storm. The expedition of Sebastian Viscaino, which anchored in the bay on December 5, 1602, was to claim this land for Spain—to include its "Costanoan" subjects.

Serra's (1770) Landing site below the Presidio hill   [GL 89-033-118]

Seasonal movements, acorn gathering, hunting and shellfish collecting continued uninterrupted until the Spanish came again in 1770, this time bringing Father Serra by sea, to meet Gaspar de Portola's overland detachment that had marched north from San Diego. The meeting point of these two expeditions was where the small creek ran into the bay, below the Costanoan knoll. This time the white men stayed and forever changed the fate of Monterey Bay's hapless original inhabitants. It also signaled the end of man's use of the bounty of this sea for his subsistence. The new lords of this coast were to set in motion the commercial use of its resources, a concept alien to the Rumsen and Esselen except for the shiny shells they traded to inland tribes.

In the century to follow, these passive "savages" were evangelized, exploited, dispersed, decimated by white men's diseases and racially absorbed into the Spanish and Mexican populations. Their vantage point above the bay had, however, quickly become the site of the conquistador's "presidio."

A VIEW FROM THE PRESIDIO

In the years since Serra's landing, the knoll that was once the sight of the Costanoan "rancheria" was to witness the establishment of Monterey as the Spanish capital of Alta California and the construction of "El Castillo," a fort at its crest with a view to the sea and the sprawling cluster of early structures on its shoreline.

In November 1818, three years before Mexican independence, the fort and harbor were brought under siege by the Argentine privateer Hippolite Bouchard. The fort's cannons accounted well for themselves, seriously damaging one of Bouchard's ships in a rare ship vs. shore-battery artillery duel, before depleting their ammunition. The town was looted and burned before Bouchard's ships set sail, the fortress having ultimately failed its protective purpose.

New England whaling ships, bound to and from ports like Lahaina, Maui, were a common sight at anchor in Monterey to replenish their provisions. The Alta California coastline was also familiar with Russian otter hunters, employing Aleuts with sealskin boats, who were joined by Spanish and American hunters to bring this widely pursued Pacific Coast species to near extinction, ironically about the time Charles Darwin was penning "Origin of Species."

On July 7, 1846, Commodore John Drake Sloat brought California under the flag of the United States when his forces put ashore to hoist the American flag at the Custom House. The Americans immediately set out to construct their own defenses on the knoll, known as Fort Mervine. Then came the gold rush to the Sierras which nearly shut Monterey down, even closing the fort in 1852. Reactivated briefly during the Civil War, it remained unused from 1865 to 1902.

The distant Hotel Del Monte, its beach-side bath house, Monterey's train depot, and the Pacific Coast Steamship Co. pier share the view from the former Costanoan knoll, and its El Castillo successor, Fort Mervine, now the Presidio of Monterey.   *C. W. J. Johnson photo, circa 1890. [GL 96-050-010]*

THE POINT PIÑOS LIGHTHOUSE

The first navigation aids for west coast shipping were approved by Congress in 1850 which allocated funds for the construction of a series of eight lighthouses on the Pacific Coast—one located at Point Piños, now Pacific Grove.

The completed lighthouse cast its beacon for the first time on February 1, 1855. In 1880 its lard oil light source was replaced by kerosene, and by electricity in 1915.

Its first light keeper, Charles Layton, was killed during its first year of operation while on a posse in pursuit of Anastacio Garcia, one of the Central Coast's most notorious outlaws. Two of its light keepers have been women: Layton's widow, Charlotte, and Mrs. Emily A. Fish, 1893, shown in photo.

PACIFIC GROVE

In 1875, a year after the arrival of rail service to the Monterey Peninsula, Reverend J. W. Ross—with generous support from landholder David Jacks— formed the Pacific Grove Retreat Association, which established a Methodist Episcopal Retreat in the wooded slopes above Point Piños.

In 1889, the Methodist summer settlement was incorporated as Pacific Grove by its permanent residents, complete with a curfew law and a fence surrounding the entire settlement. Its gate was locked each night until a prominent attorney, Judge Langford, tired of the long walk for its key chopped it down. It was never replaced.

The growth of the town soon made it an adversary of the continued Chinese occupation at China Point. In addition to the repulsive smell of drying fish and squid from the settlement, the righteous Christians of Pacific Grove became increasingly agitated over "heathen" Chinese religious ceremonies and unorthodox customs—such as the smoking of opium. Additionally, the Southern Pacific's acquisition of huge tracts of Monterey, Pacific Grove and Carmel Bay real estate from David Jacks, included prime shoreline property envisioned for development which included China Point. Bolstered by resentment and public opinion against the Chinese, in 1905 its Pacific Improvement Company ordered them off the site which they had been leasing since the 1850s.

Arson destroyed the Chinese village in 1906, resolving the objections of the good citizens of Pacific Grove. The Chinese were prevented from returning to even sift the ashes of the fire for whatever possessions survived. 1915 saw Monterey Boat Works open on part of the site. In 1918, Stanford's Hopkins Marine Station joined the boat works on the China Point site of Monterey's Chinese settlement.

This beacon is now a Pacific Grove landmark as the longest continuously operating lighthouse on the West Coast. Only San Francisco's Alcatraz light is older, but has not operated continuously.
C. K. Tuttle [GL 72-008-072]

The Methodist summer retreat that became Pacific Grove began as tent platforms, some of which actually became doll house-like wooden structures that survive today. C.K. Tuttle [73-026-025]

The Methodist summer tent cabins established with the arrival of rail service to the Peninsula soon gave way to a real town in the piney woods above Point Piños. This photo is the town gate at Lighthouse Avenue and Grand Avenue. C. W. J. Johnson photo, early 1880s. [78-006-001]

An early photograph records the Chinese settlement, its Joss House, and a junk anchored offshore. The odor from drying fish and squid was not a problem in the initial isolation of their settlement.

C. K. Tuttle [GL 72-017-130]

Few peoples on earth use more of everything they catch, grow or process than do the Chinese; virtually nothing is wasted. So it was that when the first Chinese settled in the Monterey Bay area—in the cove at Point Lobos about 1851—they must have rejoiced at the vast variety and bounty offered to their talents as experienced fishermen.

Sandy Lydon's brilliant work on the Chinese of the Monterey Bay region, "Chinese Gold," is quick to point out that the Chinese settlements at Point Lobos, "China Point" (near Cannery Row), and Pescadero (Stillwater Cove) were populated by fishing families, often having arrived directly by junk from China. Unlike other early groups immigrating to the Monterey Bay, the Chinese came as whole families and took up fishing for their own subsistence, and for drying and shipment to other Chinese enclaves in America or export to China.

Monterey's fishing industry was established by the industrious Chinese who brought with them the technique of preserving their catch by drying it for shipment, an important element in the development of this major industry made possible by Monterey's dependably dry summer months. Not since the Costanoans had anyone used the total environmental resources so thoroughly, but unfortunately the efficiency with which they did so raised both concern and an element of envy among their many critics. With a purported $200,000 annual business at the turn of the century, the Chinese became the target for more than simple racial intolerance; their diversity and adaptation to the marine resources unexploited by Japanese and European immigrants led the more resourceful of those groups into direct competition with them.

The growth of Monterey's Chinese community in the late 1880s was paralleled by the influx of other immigrant nationalities, most notably the Japanese, some of whom entered fishing as a commercial activity. Early struggles for primacy on the fishing grounds left the Chinese to adjust to the rapid success of Japanese and European nationalities using the railhead to San Francisco to market "fresh" fish from their operations near the Custom House.

Restrictive legislation and regulation of Chinese fishing and processing techniques, and rising anti-Chinese sentiment, pressured the adaptive Orientals into a commercial species not in conflict with their rapidly entrenched fishing competition: squid. It was not a commodity of concern to European immigrant fishing groups and had the advantage of being conducted at night, when their fishing operations did not conflict with their rival's use of the bay. Pacific Grove's "Feast of Lanterns" is an ironic tribute to the torches and pitchwood fires used from the Chinese sampans to attract the curious squid to their waiting seines.

Exclusionary legislation heavily restricting Chinese immigration, prohibiting naturalization, ownership of land, testimony against whites, and access to public education, provided the back-drop against which local forces were being brought to bear: they were no longer welcome on China Point.

On the evening of May 16, 1906, the Chinatown where Pacific Grove borders New Monterey, was engulfed in flames that destroyed nearly the entire shanty-like settlement—itself hosting refugees from the April 18th San Francisco earthquake and fire. This pyre signalled the end of the Chinese fishing industry. Within a year its undisbursed inhabitants negotiated for and relocated to a new and much smaller settlement on McAbee Beach on Ocean View Avenue, inside the Monterey city limits near the center of what was to become "Cannery Row."

One of the few structures to survive the fire at China Point was the Joss House. Perhaps only Trinity County's Weaverville Joss House rivals it in significance. Unfortunately, unlike its Weaverville counterpart—part of a railroad and mining Chinese presence—it did not achieve preservation as an historical monument. After the fire, it was moved to McAbee Beach where it remained until construction of the Monterey Canning Company in 1917. In March, 1942, it burned and was torn down on a Wave Street lot shared with a triplex for cannery workers, known by its inhabitants and neighbors as the "Palace Flophouse."

Monterey's coastal Chinese settlement was built right out to the water's edge, with direct access to the sheltered beach from which they launched their fishing boats. Fish were routinely dried on racks and lines within the village. It was large-scale use of the fields around the village to dry fishing catches—particularly squid—that drew objections to its smell from the ever encroaching cities of Pacific Grove and Monterey. Dan Freeman [73-035-003]

Flat-bottomed Chinese fishing boats could be pulled directly onto the beach, an advantage over Italian feluccas and other keeled boats which had to propped upright on the shoreline in Monterey's harbor (see Page 54). Fishing for squid at night, small pitchwood fires suspended in metal baskets at the prows of these boats, attracted squid into the nets of Chinese fishermen. Though some disagreement lingers, there is little doubt that the lights from China Point squid boats provided the basis for Pacific Grove's annual "Feast of Lanterns." C. K. Tuttle [GL 72-008-132]

In the early isolation of the settlement, the odor of drying squid was not a problem—but would become one with the growth of Pacific Grove.
C. E. Watkins photo, 1883. [78-050-001]

In 1879, the village was bisected by the track-bed of the Southern Pacific rail line to Pacific Grove. The division by the rail line acted as a fire break in the 1906 fire—the largest of three that struck the village since its establishment in the 1850s—and the last the Chinese would suffer. [80-007-001]

Note China Point's granite promontory rising behind the main street of the settlement prior to the fire on May 16, 1906. [78-037-001]

After the fire of May 16th, 1906, guards from the Pacific Improvement Company attempt to prevent Chinese from returning to salvage or rebuild their settlement. The Southern Pacific had other plans for it that did not involve continued occupation by the Chinese. [81-062-014]

The McAbee Chinatown, circa 1911, with its reduction plant (with smokestack), and on the far right, the Joss House—in its second location—spared from the fire at China Point by its separation from the main settlement by the Southern Pacific track bed .   *J. K. Oliver photo.* [73-012-003]

Quock Mui in a photo from the mid-1920s, standing on her front porch at 774 Wave Street. Mary Chin Lee photo [86-091-001]

After the China Point fire of 1906, a much smaller Chinese settlement was created on a beach closer to Monterey, as its owner, San Franciscan, John A. McAbee, leased parcels to the Chinese that decided to remain and rebuild. McAbee's seaside bathing and boat rental venture suffered from Monterey's dependable summer fog and lack of attendance when an opportunity came to lease to the displaced Chinese. A new settlement, much resembling the old, began to take form on the former Portuguese whaling beach. The odor of drying fish and squid created an immediate problem in the more heavily residential area of the coast than had been the case at China Point. Objections to the Chinese presence by neighbors like estate owner, James A. Murray, did not prevent the gradual growth of the settlement. Squid drying was finally banned in Monterey's city limits and that process was moved to Tarpey Flats near present Monterey Municipal Airport. Because of the dwindling Chinese workforce, the squid field work was done largely by Caucasian laborers desperate for work.

The most significant person emerging from the Chinese community during this period was a cannery worker known as "Spanish Mary." Born at Point Lobos in 1859, Quock Mui moved to China Point and raised her family. Her facility for languages earned her wide regard among the area's emigrants who entrusted her to interpret contracts and official documents for them in a white-American dominated legal and business system.

In the 1920s she moved into the neighborhood above Ocean View Avenue, referred to as the "Third Cannery Row Chinatown." Her home at 774 Wave Street is preserved as an historical site dedicated to her role in the rich and colorful Chinese heritage of Cannery Row.

Her talented brother, Quock Ah Tuck Lee, became a skilled and highly regarded tide pool research species collector for studies at Hopkins Marine Station and for Ed Ricketts at the dawn of marine sciences on the California Coast at Monterey.

WHAT A DIFFERENCE A TRAIN MAKES

The original narrow-gauge trackway laid the nearly twenty miles between Salinas and Monterey in 1874, was a Granger's challenge to the rail freight monopoly of the Southern Pacific's "Big Four"–Crocker, Stanford, Huntington and Hopkins. The narrow-gauge system connected the Salinas wheat and agricultural markets to a rail pier in Monterey for shipment by sea. It also enabled the growing Monterey fishing industry to connect to major markets for its "fresh" fish up the line toward in San Francisco. Italian and Portuguese operators in Monterey did not ice or gut the catch for shipment; the waste in spoiled fish had the effect of keeping prices up.

Although the Monterey & Salinas Valley Railroad failed within five years—primarily due to winter bridge failures over the Salinas River—it demonstrated the market it could serve and its valuable access to the scenic Monterey Peninsula, which was being targeted for large scale tourism development as a resort destination.

When Southern Pacific bought the bankrupt railroad at auction, it matched the acquisition with a purchase of over 6,000 acres of the Monterey Peninsula (including large parts of the City of Monterey, all of the Methodist Retreat of Pacific Grove, the Del Monte Forest (now Pebble Beach), and parts of Carmel Valley) from David Jacks, to complement and support Crocker's dream of constructing "the most elegant seaside establishment in the world." Southern Pacific laid the spur line to the Peninsula from its main line at Castroville. The doorway to the Monterey Bay area had been opened wide to tourism and large scale land development.

David Jack (1822–1909) acquired most of the Monterey Peninsula at a highly questionable tax auction of City of Monterey lands and grants in 1859, enabling its later sale to the Southern Pacific.
I. W. Taber photo 1895 [2000-024-002]

The iron horses of Southern Pacific brought the wealthy to the Hotel Del Monte and immigrants to the Monterey fishing industry who prospered with a rail connection to San Francisco.
C. K. Tuttle [GL 72-008-054]

The hub of wealth and social activity of the Monterey Peninsula, the lavish hotel was to have a major impact on the economics of tourism and residential elegance.　　　　　　　　　　　　　　　*C. W. J. Johnson photo, circa 1885.* [79-106-008]

The magnificent Hotel Del Monte was constructed in less than half a year and opened its doors on June 3, 1880 to throngs of prominent and wealthy patrons from around the world. They were fetched by carriage from the hotel's own "Del Monte Station" on the new Southern Pacific line completed from the main line at Castroville. Its over 160 acres boasted exotic gardens, a lake, four heated swimming pools, a polo field, amusements and accommodations fit for royalty.

Perhaps its most unusual entertainment was a "seventeen-mile drive" through the crumbling adobes of Monterey, past the curious Chinatown to the Pacific Grove gate, and on to the "pebbled beach" on Carmel Bay. The original drive passed through the Chinese fishing family settlement at Pescadero, where Jung San Choy and his family set up one of Monterey's first souvenir stands in 1881, selling abalone shells and other curios to the more adventurous of the grand hotel's guests. The rustic log Del Monte Lodge began as a rest stop and place to eat while horses were watered or changed for the return trip to the hotel. Occasional side-tours took in Carmel or the Mission on the way back over the Carmel hill to Monterey.

The lavish hotel was destroyed by fire on April 1st, 1887, and rebuilt from its original plans. Its Lodge at Pebble Beach on Carmel Bay was lost to fire in 1917 and reopened with adjoining lodging in 1919—the same year its golf course opened on the plateaus above Pebble Beach, a panorama which no longer included the Chinese.

The Del Monte Hotel's beach-side bath house, only one of a vast number of entertainments provided the guests of the hotel. Another was the Seventeen Mile Drive. [82-003-016]

The Seventeen-Mile Drive passed through old Monterey, as seen in this view from the roof of the Custom House looking up Alvarado Street and Calle Principal, in this photo by C. W. J. Johnson, 1893. The two-story adobe Pacific Building at the right survives. [GL 89-033-127]

The world-famous "Seventeen-Mile Drive" circa 1910, when horse drawn carriages had been replaced by automobiles like the "Royal Tourister" touring car seen in this photo taken near Cypress Point, not far from the early Lodge at Pebble Beach on Carmel Bay. K. Tuttle [GL 72-008-045]

A souvenir stand—one of Monterey's earliest—was set up by Jung San Choy and his family beside their house on the Seventeen Mile Drive, on the shoreline above what is now Stillwater Cove.
Joseph K. Oliver photo [78-041-002]

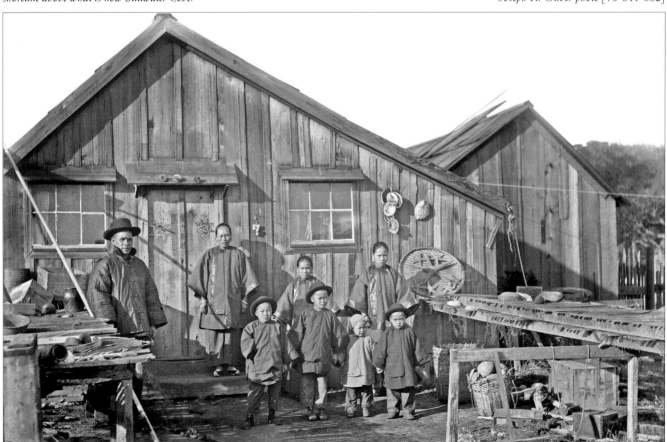

The home and family of Jung San Choy, leader of the Chinese fishing village at Pescadero on Carmel Bay. The Chinese had fished Carmel Bay from their earlier settlement at Point Lobos since 1851.
C. K. Tuttle [GL 72-017-084]

Another portion of the Pescadero Chinese fishing village from an 1880s photograph of what is now the Beach and Tennis Club of the Lodge at Pebble Beach. Joseph K. Oliver photo. [71-018-003]

The gentleman in the derby in this 1911 R. J. Arnold photo of an arrival at the log Lodge at Pebble Beach is photographer Dan Freeman. Auto travel greatly facilitated access to the shores of Carmel Bay from Monterey and the Hotel Del Monte. [82-029-011]

The graphic origin of a name: the pebbled beach on Carmel Bay. The 17-Mile Drive continued along the plateaus above the beaches nearly to Carmel before climbing the hilly return trip to the Hotel Del Monte. Golfers should recognize this photo location as the 18th Fairway at Pebble Beach. An extended route took in the village of Carmel-By-The-Sea and the Carmel Mission near where the Carmel River runs into Carmel Bay.   C. K. Tuttle [GL 72-017-070]

Early Carmel developed by L. Frank Devendorf and Frank Powers was a curiosity worth a side trip from the Seventeen Mile Drive. By 1923 Carmel -by-the-Sea was becoming both quaint and civilized, though paving had not yet arrived on Ocean Avenue.
Lewis Josselyn photo. [71-001-0484]

26

The restoration of Mission San Carlos Borromeo del Rio Carmelo began with an 1883 donation by Mrs. Leland Stanford. Lewis Josselyn captures the restoration progress and a Pierce-Arrow in this 1919 photo. [71-001-CM0]

The sheltered cove, first settled by Chinese, used briefly by the shore-whaling Portuguese, became a major Japanese abalone diving and canning operation.

ABALONE AND THE JAPANESE

Japanese immigrants arriving in the early 1890s were predominantly farmers and part-time fishermen. It was pioneer labor contractor and businessman Otosaburo Noda who reported back to Japan of the coast's plentiful abalone, particularly in the Carmel Bay area. The Japanese government sent Gennosuke Kodani, a marine biologist with extensive experience in hard hat diving technology and credentials that would establish the Monterey abalone industry, to confirm Noda's reports. Arriving in 1896, he completed a reconnaissance of the coast for the ideal location, which he found at Point Lobos—along with its owner A.M. Allan, who became a partner in the venture.

At first abalone diving at Point Lobos began with "free diving" without insulated suits or helmets, as practiced in Japan. But the Pacific's frigid temperatures at Monterey quickly demanded the introduction of Japanese hard-hat divers, a first for this technology on the Central Coast. Kodani drew his divers from Japan's Chiba Prefecture, near

Tokyo, which had just suffered a major fire in its abalone industry. Expert hard-hat divers were eager to join in the new American abalone diving venture.

The Kodani operation began by shipping dried abalone. Around 1902, equipment from the Gayette abalone cannery at Wild Cat Cove in the Carmel Highlands may have been acquired for the initial canning of cubed and minced abalone for export—supplemented by fishing for salmon and sardines for delivery to Monterey's canneries. The cutting and pounding of abalone prior to processing was also conducted on what was to become known as Fisherman's Wharf in Monterey's harbor. The Japanese soon established a solid presence in the new canning industry on the Central Coast. Along with it, however, came the kinds of prejudicial treatment and regulation so familiar to the Chinese before them.

The Japanese led the way for later American hard-hat development on the coast, skills that would prove indispensable to the growth and capacity of the Monterey canning industry.

At the end of the 1920s, off-loading the towed barges of the early lampara fleet by steel buckets up and down cables to the canneries proved unworkable for unloading the large new purse-seiners rapidly replacing them. A new system for off-loading the huge new purse seiners was needed. The inventive genius of Norwegian-born cannery operator, Knut Hovden, was called upon again and he delivered: he devised a system of sturdy

Dan Freeman's photo shows the defunct bunker at Coal Chute Point, the Kodani residence, and the whitewashed Japanese bunkhouse, 1905. [73-035-002]

wood-beam hoppers with underwater pipelines to the canneries into which the purse-seiners brailed their loads. Large turbine pumps in each cannery literally sucked the sardines ashore. The plan required brave, hardy and skilled hard-hat divers working underwater to anchor the floating hoppers, to bolt together, install and maintain the large pipes to each cannery pump house. The divers were not Japanese, but their technology and techniques provided the means to command Monterey's eventual claim as "Sardine Capital of the World" during WW II.

The Japanese community also played a very major role in the canning industry workforce, specializing in the cutting operation. Japanese became a major factor in the economic life both Monterey and Cannery Row. There were also a small number of purse-seiners in the Monterey sardine fleet owned and operated by Japanese Americans with Japanese crews.

Before the closure of Point Lobos abalone operations in 1935, there were as many as eighteen diving boats, each with a crew of four—some operating as far south as Moro Bay. For a time the flagship of this Point Lobos flotilla was the "Ocean Queen," a sizeable rum runner's boat abandoned in hot pursuit at the cove and later bought by Kodani at auction from the government during Prohibition.

Prior to 1941, most of the fish processors and fish markets on Monterey's Fisherman's Wharf were Japanese owned and operated. Wartime expropriation of these businesses and internment of Monterey's Japanese American citizens during World War II ended the Japanese as a major influence in Monterey's fishing economy. They were also unable to recover their expropriated businesses after WW II internment.

The rum-running Ocean Queen, which became the flagship of the Japanese abalone flotilla operating from the cove at Point Lobos. 1924 photo [83-046-001]

29

A dive boat is towed from the protected cove, past the cannery at "Whaler's Cove," a name surviving both Chinese and Japanese occupations of the cove.
C. K. Tuttle 1902 [GL 72-008-0176]

This leading hard-hat diver, Aoki, prepares for the cold, dangerous work of harvesting abalone below. Hard-hat diving immediately replaced unsuccessfull un-insulated initial free-diving.   *Lewis Josselyn [71-01-PL-06]*

Aoki goes over the side of this dive boat with his abalone net decades before hard-hat diving becomes indispensable as a component of the Monterey canning industry's fish-hoppers and underwater pipelines.   *Lewis Josselyn [71-01-PL-05]*

The new technology of hard hat diving for abalone was to have important ramifications for the young sardine industry which was also to become dependent on diving technology.   *Lewis Josselyn photo, 1916 [71-001-PL6]*

Across Whaler's Cove from the Point Lobos Canning Company cannery, Carmelo Land and Coal Company's unprofitable Coal Chute Point venture was adapted for drying abalone, as seen in this September, 1905, E. A. Cohen photo.   *[77-003-202]*

Gennosuke Kodani (seated center) and crew with drying abalone on Coal Chute Point. Spoilage of sacked abalone in shipment to Japan was a disaster. Kodani quickly adopted canning, introduced by the Gayette brother's abalone cannery at nearby Wild Cat Creek Cove.   C. K. Tuttle [GL 72-008-175]

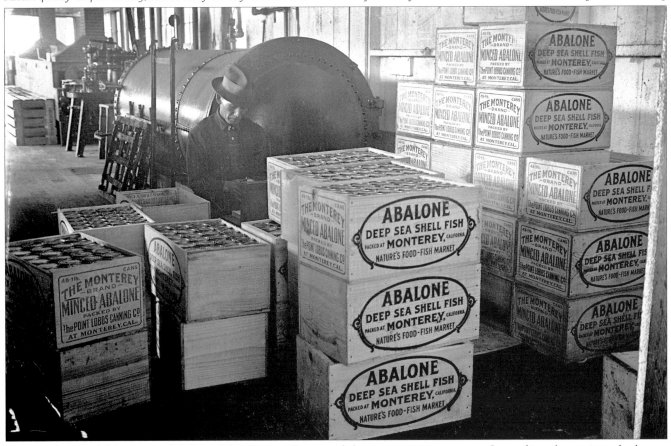

Lewis Josselyn recorded the interior of the Point Lobos Canning Company abalone canning operation, 1916. It was this early canning technology at Point Lobos that launched the first canning operation (also Japanese) on the uninhabited shore line of old Ocean View Avenue in 1902.   [71-01-PL11]

Portuguese shore-whalers flensing a humpback whale on McAbee Beach in the 1890s. Kerosene would doom such whaling at Monterey, vacating this once remote beach for other ventures. The coastal steamer "Gypsy" is underway in the background.　　　*C. K. Tuttle photo. [GL 72-017-036]*

Whaling in the Monterey Bay dates back to the Spanish period when New Bedford deep-water whaling ships dropped anchor in the harbor at Monterey to resupply for their global ship-based assaults on the migrating giants. The gray and humpback varieties were so plentiful, and migrated so close to the Monterey's peninsula shorelines–as they did in the Azores Islands of the Atlantic–in 1854, Captain John Pope Davenport organized the first of Monterey's "shore whaling" enterprises. Key to Davenport's success was the recruitment of available and experienced Azorean Portuguese whalers, particularly the many with shore whaling experience from their native Atlantic islands.

In the decades following Monterey's depopulation by the gold rush, the growth of several Portuguese-manned shore whaling companies must have provided what little excitement could be seen along the shores of the former Spanish and Mexican–and now American–port. Longboats were sailed and rowed from shore to meet the hapless targets of harpoon and bomb-lance. A successful strike with the "Greener's (harpoon) gun" ensured a wild ride as the longboat was dragged great distances at high speed behind the wounded whale before it tired and could be dispatched and towed back to shore.

The "try-works" on the shores below Monterey's first first Whaling Station and Jack Swan's place, near the Custom House, and later at McAbee Beach on what is now Cannery Row, rendered the blubber into oil as the whales were flensed on the beaches. The stench of boiling whale blubber was an olfactory fact of life in early Monterey, as whale bones became piled high nearly the length of the beach at Monterey. The smell of this process would portend the stench of Monterey's sardine industry reduction process to come.

Kerosene replaced whale oil by the turn of the century as Portuguese shore-whalers had to turn to fishing and farming.

1907 post card of McAbee Beach as a seaside resort.　　*[83-080-004]*

September 28, 1905, the coastal steamer "Gypsy" went aground at McAbee Beach, with a ship-load of beer successfully salvaged.　　*[84-004-006]*

33

The Tevis Estate, inspired by the grandeur of the Hotel Del Monte, occupied 1000 feet of coastline. The grand Casa de las Olas, "House of the Waves," was built by Hugh Tevis as a summer house for his young Denver socialite bride. It is now the site of a luxury hotel. E. K. Baker [79-043-002]

Certainly influenced by the stately splendor of the grand Hotel Del Monte–and with the added advantage of a sweeping panorama of the Monterey Bay–a magnificent estate was created in 1901 on the shores of a sandy beach on Ocean Avenue (renamed Ocean View in the 1920s). Hugh Tevis, son of wealthy Lloyd Tevis, assumed full-time management of the family investments, to include property in Monterey upon the death of his father in 1889. In 1880, his father had declared the opulent Hotel Del Monte the official family summer residence and he entertained lavishly there for many years.

Hugh Tevis' first wife Alice died after the birth of their daughter, Alice Boalt Tevis. Raised by her grandmother, she traveled and vacationed frequently with her father. It was on such a trip, staying at the Del Monte, that she met Cornelia Baxter, a "princess" whom she insisted her father meet.

The gorgeous eighteen-year-old debutante from a wealthy Denver family had been sent to the Hotel Del Monte to recuperate from typhoid. The romance that ensued soon resulted in their engagement in March and their marriage in April, 1901.

Hugh's wedding present to his young bride, intended as a summer home, was scheduled for a September completion. They were on a trip to the Orient shopping for furnishings for the estate as it neared completion that Hugh Tevis died in Yokohama from appendicitis. Cornelia and her relatives moved into the palatial estate in September, 1901, where she remained until her son Hugh was born in San Francisco the following February. She was unhappy and lonely in the mansion and decided it would be sold. "Casa del las Olas" (House of the Waves) passed quickly through the hands of David Jack who sold it in 1904 to mining magnate James A. Murray.

Although not a "Copper King" himself, James Murray ascended into the ranks of Montana mining millionaires with a Midas touch in his tough but honest financial dealings. He was an occasional visitor and heavy spender at the Hotel Del Monte and his wealth required a suitable residence as he eyed Monterey for his retirement with his second wife, Mary, and her son, Stuart Haldorn. His was not a full retirement as he kept up his financial interests while embarking into the arena of local Monterey art and history patronage.

Perhaps having been a mining man kept him from objecting to a growing number of nearby storage tanks and the Associated Oil Company pier that now encroached the view from the "Murray Mansion." But how could Murray have possibly known the future consequences of the archaic sardine canning experiments in the Booth cannery at the harbor, or at the rudimentary sardine packing shed toward McAbee Beach that would become the Pacific Fish Company. Monterey's new cannery construction along the once remote coastal road was well underway by Murray's death in 1921.

By early 1941 the estate, surrounded by the noise and smell of cannery expansion, succumbed to that pressure. It was sold to Angelo Lucido, owner of the San Carlos Cannery, who soon subdivided the property for sale to more cannery and reduction plant development accelerated by the onset of World War II. The halcyon days of the Tevis-Murray estate were over; it was demolished in 1944 at the peak of wartime cannery expansion for wartime food production. The features of the Tevis-Murray Estate became unrecognizable; nothing remained of the estate's original grandeur and elegance. It's time would return, but not again soon. Not on the Old Row.

The Wu Family's stylish Ocean View Hotel and restaurant built in 1927 on the former McAbee Beach site of the Second Chinatown after the 1906 fire. Neil De Vaughn's restaurant helped launch the Cannery Row Renaissance from here in the early 1950s. 1934 A. C. Heidrick photo courtesy of James Wu [86-051-001]

Monterey and Cannery Row Entrepreneur Maen Chang Wu seated in his fashionable oceanfront restaurant. Photo courtesy of James Wu [86-051-002]

The Portuguese shore-whalers were long gone from the beach which became known as McAbee Beach at the turn of the new century. Time stood almost still on this shoreline almost since the gold rush. Little disturbed the tranquility of the nearby Tevis-Murray estate until the fire that destroyed the major Chinese settlement at China Point in 1906.

The fire triggered several important changes. The fire dispersed a large portion of the once thriving Chinese enclave at China Point in Pacific Grove into several new locations located within Monterey. It also forever ended the Chinese participation in the further development of Monterey's fishing industry. Notably, it also resulted in the successful negotiation for a new but smaller Chinatown inside the Monterey city limits at McAbee Beach.

John McAbee, a Scotsman, had developed a seaside tent-cottage and boat rental business just prior to the turn of the century. Visitors braved the chilly waters of Monterey Bay and too often endured Monterey's famously foggy summers. It was not a profitable venture and struggled through several lean seasons before succumbing as the last of the beach's recreational enterprises for almost a hundred years. The nearly vacant beach would become Chinese, over the strenuous objections of James Murray and other local dignitaries, as China Point's refugees obtained leases from the Scot for a new settlement.

By 1910 the industrious "newcomers" had erected a somewhat more conventional-appearing settlement above the beach, facing Ocean View Avenue. Included were the Joss House, which had escaped the 1906 fire, and the Monterey Fishing and Canning Company, engaged almost entirely in reducing fish heads and offal from Booth and Pacific Fish Co. to fertilizer —Monterey's first major "reduction" plant. Now inside the Monterey city limits, the Chinese were prohibited from drying squid at McAbee's and moved that operation to the highway toward Salinas, outside city jurisdiction. As more Chinese moved out of fishing, an Oriental quarter grew up at Franklin and Washington Streets in downtown Monterey, containing both Chinese and Japanese. The oriental style Ocean View Hotel was built in 1927 above the vacated beach by the Wu Family, Chinese from San Francisco who owned

the Bay State Cafe on Alvarado Street (Page 54 photo) in Monterey prior to their investment on Ocean View Avenue.

In 1929, an annex to the hotel across the street was built as the Marina Apartments. It's matching tile "dragon roof" survives today, though the hotel does not. In a matter of years from its opening it became one of the brothels for which the Cannery Row district was becoming notorious. It survives today as the most prominent reminder of the once major influence of the Chinese on the character of Ocean View Avenue.

Since John Steinbeck's 1945 portrayal of old Cannery Row in the 1930s the Marina Apartments has been a visual and nostalgic delight for many visitors. Certain locals knew the upstairs of the building as the bordello of Rose Giavanelli, a bouncer in particular by the name of Charlie Nonella–to whom this book is dedicated. After WW II and the onset of the increasing numbers of curious Steinbeck readers interested in seeing the locales in his "Cannery Row" a sign was hung over the doorway of a cafe in the street level of the building proclaiming "Bear Flag Inn." It was an unfounded claim but who was to know? Its misleading claim has, however, pleased an unknowing share of the Steinbeck seekers who did not. It survived into the present as a radio station and is now shops and services for Monterey's biggest attraction, The Old Row.

The Ocean View Hotel and its Annex on the right, the Marina Apartments (built in 1929), many years later during the demise of the canning industry's reign on the Monterey waterfront. Jem photo [91-002-001]

PACIFIC GROVE AT PLAY

The Chinese and their squid drying had been vanquished by fire; their move to New Monterey's McAbee Beach had ended the only other nearby boating and seaside recreation. Landowner, William Smith, had dynamited the beach at Pacific Grove into existence at Point Aulon before Japanese entrepreneur and abalone industry pioneer, Otosaburo Noda, constructed a Japanese tea house and garden in 1904. It joined an earlier structure on the bluff above the beach, Stanford University's Hopkins Seaside Laboratory. The laboratory opened on the point in 1892, a gift of Timothy Hopkins and the Southern Pacific's development arm, the Pacific Improvement Company. The Hopkins Seaside Laboratory was the first such research facility to study the marine life on the west coast. Pacific Grove took on new life as other entertainment and tourist establishments followed at what was called Lover's Point.

Among its notable attractions was a glass-bottomed boat concession, a bath house, a heated salt-water swimming pool, auditorium and photography studio.

After the 1906 fire at China Point, the dilemma as to what to do with the land, already mapped for the development of residential home sites, was resolved. Pacific Improvement Company donated the land to the University of California. By 1918, in an interesting transfer of assets, Hopkins Seaside Laboratory had relocated from Lovers Point to China Point and reopened as the Hopkins Marine Station of Stanford University.

Unfortunately, the curriculum did not deal with the fate of either salmon...or the sardine.

IT ALL STARTED WITH SALMON

Monterey's early commercial fishermen were by stock a hardy and independent group, in many ways reflecting the state of the industry of the times. The Chinese were doing a brisk business to their San Francisco and overseas markets. The first salmon caught by trolling in Monterey Bay induced a concerted hook-and-line fleet of sailing skiffs, mostly Japanese, to pursue this magnificent species commercially. Of all the market fish varieties being caught, none was to be more important to the turn-of-the-century Monterey Bay area economy than salmon.

Salmon buyers ventured south to Monterey in the early 1890s to buy salmon for packing plants at San Francisco and the Sacramento River. One such visitor was Frank E. Booth, president of the Sacramento River Packer's Association, who by 1896 concluded that the salmon supply warranted the construction of a local packing house.

Autumn of 1907 at Lovers Point, Pacific Grove. The swan-necked glass bottomed boats, built by Russell Sprague in 1886, and the Japanese Tea House (by pioneer Japanese developer, Otosaburo Noda) dominate the point and its entertainments. C. K. Tuttle [GL 72-008-091]

Hopkins Seaside Laboratory, (1890s photo) at Lovers Point until moved to China Point in 1917 as Hopkins Marine Station of Stanford University, on property declined by the University of California after the San Francisco earthquake and fire of 1906. C. K. Tuttle [GL 72-008-080]

Booth built, but shortly closed, an experimental salmon canning shed adjacent to the Pacific Coast Steamship Company pier as Monterey's fishermen spurned contracts to supply Booth and accepted higher bids from San Francisco agents. Booth's venture was forced to close due to the lack of fishermen's cooperation. Monterey's fishermen were rewarded for their lack of judgement as the price paid for fish plunged after Booth closed his first canning venture at Monterey.

Booth tried again in 1901, but was no longer the only packer at Monterey. San Franciscan H. R. Robbins had constructed a small wharf, complete with a smoke house and warehouse, adjacent to the steamship pier. Both operated successfully, but with much difficulty in 1902 before Booth's canning operation was destroyed by fire. Robbins' operation was struggling with its own difficulties and was unable to take advantage of Booth's misfortune. Robbins' experiments in reduction of scraps and salmon waste, however, proved to be an interesting and somewhat lucrative sideline—but not profitable enough to save him. Booth returned in 1903, buying out the Robbins operation and set out to enlarge it. Monterey's fishermen also finally cooperated.

This early postcard clearly explains the initial interests in Monterey as a promising fishing port. It was salmon like this that brought the fish buyers to Monterey from San Francisco and the Sacramento River, later to experiment in canning salmon at its source in Monterey. [86-012-004]

Salmon put Monterey on the commercial map at the turn of the century and another postcard clearly reflects the bounty of its beautiful bay waters, with 7,000 salmon caught on hook-and-line in a single day by a fleet of predominantly Japanese sailing skiffs. Edward H. Mitchell (Publisher) [78-062-001]

Pioneer Monterey salmon and sardine packer, Frank E. Booth, "Father of the Monterey Sardine Industry."   *George Habenicht Studios* [78-047-001]

Booth's cannery and its Crescent Brand Sardines proclaimed on its roof sign. Its pollution of the harbor with fish waste and its industrial appearance in the heart of scenic Monterey's harbor did little to endear it to non-fishing and canning interests. All other canneries were made to locate elsewhere—which meant out the dangerously rocky coastline near McAbee Beach and China Point. [87-032-001]

A view of the Booth cannery from Fisherman's Wharf. As with the sardine factories to come, form followed function in the design and construction of Monterey's rapidly expanding fish packing industry. Additional construction of that expansion of the sardine industry, however, was banned from Monterey's harbor, forcing all subsequent canneries to locate along the rocky coastline toward China Point. Chester Toombs 1914 [85-019-079]

A photo of the crew at Frank Booth's cannery in July, 1914. His talented Norwegian manager, Knut Hovden, is on the far right, holding a small dog.

F. C. Swain [92-012-006]

Lampara nets spread to dry at "Ferrante's Landing" adjacent to Fisherman's Wharf. Maintenance of the cotton nets was critical to the fishing industry and their care and repair was of paramount importance. Major net repair was done during the week of the full moon each month of the season (August to February) when fish could not be spotted by their florescence at night due to the moon's reflection on the bay.

A. C. Heidrick circa 1911 [83-082-023]

THE UNSUNG ORIGIN

The entry of Booth's "Monterey Packing Company" consolidation of 1903 into the fish packing business was preceded a year by a rudimentary canning-shed operation begun on the rocky New Monterey coastline. Harry Malpas and Otosaburo Noda, from the Point Lobos Canning Company, opened the first canning operation on Ocean View Avenue. The small- scale "Monterey Fishing and Canning Company" opened in March, 1902, initially packing abalone and salmon. It struggled with the same erratic supplies of fish as Booth and Robbins, but operated with far fewer reserves.

Booth's general manager since 1902 was replaced by the young Norwegian canning specialist, Knut Hovden, in 1905. James A. Madison, who had joined a San Francisco canning company returned in 1907 and with Joseph Nichols negotiated the purchase of the financially troubled packing business of Harry Malpas. Another of the investors was Bernard Senderman of Pittsburg. On February 14, 1908, the "Pacific Fish Company" was born — the first major cannery on Ocean View Avenue.

"Cannery" requires some explanation and in many ways the Pacific Fish Company is a typical early profile. The delivery of fish was accomplished at a pier, constructed as far out over the rocky shoreline as possible. Fish were cut by hand to remove heads, tails and offal. They were then split and spread to drain and dry on wooden "flakes," or slats. Large flat metal baskets of "flaked" fish were then drawn through long troughs of boiling peanut oil ("French frying"), drained again, packed into cans and hand soldered closed. Labeling and boxing for warehousing and shipment completed the process. With some variation, it was common to all the early Monterey canneries. A gifted man was to change all that.

A 1911 crew photo of the draining and drying of cut sardines on "flakes" prior to being "French fried" (French Method) and canned. [81-014-001]

Early post card with sardines in metal baskets about to be drawn through troughs of boiling peanut oil to cook the sardines. M. Rieder [79-084-001]

The coastline's first packing operation, Monterey Fishing and Canning Company (1902), became Pacific Fish Company in 1908. [83-041-001]

41

A view from Wave Street shows Monterey Boatworks and the Agassiz Building of Hopkins Marine Station—on the former Chinatown site—and the early

THE PRINCE AND SOON KING

In 1905 the most important man in Monterey's sardine saga took a position with Booth's awkward and poorly mechanized canning operation at the harbor. The young Knut Hovden, a talented graduate of the Norwegian Fisheries College, had immigrated from the North Sea canning industry due to a serious respiratory problem. He brought with him both experience in an advanced canning technology and a gift of inventive genius. The archaic canning procedures he found in Monterey gave him a challenge and opportunity to apply both.

A self emptying "purse-bottom brailing net" was one of his first applied solutions to the arduous unloading of sardines from the lighters (barges) in which they were delivered to the cannery. The canning itself was to benefit enormously from his invention of a mechanical sealer-solderer, permitting an astonishing increase in production capacity. His almost immediate impact on the capacity of Booth's processing was unmatched, however, by a corresponding improvement in the increased capture and delivery of sardines. Both local fishermen and their clumsy gill nets were unsuitable to the expansion of production capacity Hovden had made possible.

The impasse was to be broken by another man of vision and "appropriate technology," a respected Sicilian fisherman from Booth's Sacramento River operation. Pietro Ferrante represented both the tough Sicilian work ethic and the intelligence to apply a familiar technique utilized by his Mediterranean ancestors — the "lampara" net. Unlike the clumsy and inefficient gill net, which was dragged into a school of sardines which were caught in it by their gills and required removal by hand after capture, the "lightning" net in the 1907 experiments at Monterey encircled the sardines and was then quickly closed at its ends to entrap its catch. The sardines were concentrated in the "bag" of the net as it was pulled in by hand, and were then brailed into the lighters towed behind the lampara boats. Booth's new canning capacity would soon be matched by a substantial improvement in the delivery of sardines — by Sicilians who knew how to conduct the lampara technique. So would begin the Sicilian mastery of the Monterey sardine fishing industry.

Hovden was soon happily seeking ways to keep canning capacity up with the rapidly burgeoning delivery rate, a situation challenging his inventiveness and an opportunity he eagerly pursued. His processing prowess at Booth's was to become legend and the opportunity to employ his innovations in his own canning facility became a carefully quiet inevitability as he assumed ever larger yet troublesome roles in the Booth operation. It is certainly appropriate that Frank Booth should be called the "Father of the sardine industry," but the young Knut Hovden would soon be its "King."

By 1915 it had become evident to Hovden that his once grateful and cooperative employer, Frank Booth, was stubbornly resisting changes and improvements he sought in the further development of his processing techniques. Those interests included his enthusiasm for the potentially lucrative reduction and sardine by-product business. Without Booth's cooperation, he ventured into a small reduction development which proved a profitable sideline to the existing canning process. That initiative seems to have been the last straw and the two powerful canning personas soon parted company.

42

cannery of the Hovden Food Products, Corp. at the Pacific Grove end of Ocean View Avenue, circa 1918.　　　A. C. Heidrick [85-012-001]

Max N. Schaefer, a vigorous and innovative businessman, was further convinced that reduction could be a major part of the industry and developed full-scale reduction as a separate industrial enterprise. His plant in San Francisco's San Pablo Bay provided the model for his "Monterey Fish Products Company," which opened in 1915 on Cannery Row.

Hovden submitted his resignation in November, 1915, and with the support of local financier and real estate man, T. A. Work, opened the "Hovden Cannery" at the north end of Ocean View Avenue on July 7,1916. Once Prince, the King had now arrived.

Hovden's ambitious assault on the "Silver Tide" of Monterey Bay helped propel the industry into new methods of cooking fish by steam, and then by steam with the fish sealed in their cans. World War I arrived as the Monterey canning industry emerged from its infancy at the prefect time to meet the world-wide demand for war-time rations. Disruption of the North Sea fishery in both World Wars would provide Monterey the investment incentives to process nearly unlimited amounts of a seemingly endless resource for a world at war. It also spelled doom for archaic processing techniques.

Knut Hovden, soon to be the "King of Cannery Row." [2003-053-001]

"Salachini" dried, salt-pack sardines displayed with canned anchovy in an unidentified packing operation. This "Old World" method of preserving fish was pursued by La Esperanza Packing Company, which eventually became Ed Ricketts' Pacific Biological Laboratories.　　　[99-071-001]

In 1918, Point Lobos canner Alexander M. Allan, and fellow Scot, George Harper, entered the fish packing industry in Monterey at the height of World War I, with their architecturally distinctive Monterey Canning Company at Prescott Avenue and Ocean View Avenue. A. C. Heidrick [86-060-001]

THE STARTING GUN

Assuming a position at the head of the pack he would never relinquish, Hovden's entry into the sardine packing industry could hardly have come at a better time. The "Great War" was to shut down the North Sea fishery, leaving Monterey's inexpensive, high-protein sardine pack in high demand as a wartime ration. By war's end, Booth, Pacific Fish, and Hovden canneries would be joined by California Fisheries Company, a Japanese export firm; Bayside Cannery near Hovden's; Monterey Canning Company, owned by George Harper and A. M. Allan of Point Lobos abalone canning; San Xavier Canning Co. near the Tevis-Murray estate; what was to become Carmel Canning Company, for Bernard Senderman, an early partner in Pacific Fish Company; the E. B. Gross Cannery near the Tevis-Murray Estate; and a brick reduction plant on Wave Street for the late entry of Frank Booth to the by-products business, joining Max Schaefer's Monterey Fish Products Co. in major reduction processing.

Cannery Row's wartime production would grow from 75,000 cases in 1915 to 1,400,000 cases in 1918; the price per case rose from $2.14 to $7.50

through that same period. The effective result of World War I on Cannery Row was to provide the industry the investment incentive to develop and mechanize the canning industry at Monterey. It was also an important step in helping overcome the stiff resistance in world markets to the large Pacific cousin of the much smaller and widely accepted Atlantic Sardine. In the United States a domestic market had hardly existed. This unprecedented wartime bonanza was, of course, too good to last; recession set in as the guns cooled.

Perhaps quaint by current standards, the rugged and highly competitive sardine industry constructed most of its canneries and warehouses with strictly functional design, although some, like the architecturally ornate Monterey Canning company and the Carmel Canning, bore artistic branding.

Carmel Canning proclaims its "Ben-Sen" brand, named after its builder, Ben Senderman, who sold out before its completed construction. The "cross-overs" are covered conveyors from warehouse to cannery. [83-041-002]

A LOOK AROUND AT CHANGING TIMES

A glimpse down Cannery Row in the aftermath of World War I would show a boomtown of corrugated canneries perched over a rocky coastline, unloading sardines from off-shore by cable and bucket — 600 pounds at a time. Although canning had been significantly mechanized, labor continued a major factor in production.

In an age before telephones in the working class home, the cannery workers were called to work by cannery whistle; each cannery had a distinct pitch and pattern. Working hours were dictated by the arrival and size of each day's catch. Work itself was generally cold, wet and smelly, in drafty, beam and plank and corrugated tin canneries where the din of steam, cascading cans and the roar of equipment often drowned out an orchestra of international languages spoken in Chinese and Spanish and Japanese in the cutting rooms and sheds — the Spanish, Portuguese, Sicilian, and English of the canning lines — and the shouts, grunts and curses of the warehousing crews.

Monterey's initial displeasure with the odors from Robbins' early salmon reduction experiments around 1902 were merely memories. But the smell of reduction would become, in the decade of the twenties, a problem of major proportions. The Chinese at McAbee had led the Row into reduction and its wrenching smell, augmented by Hovden's similar interests and the success of Max Schaefer's leadership in the processing technique. Even the stubborn Frank Booth had succumbed to its profits and utility. The net effect was a well-earned reputation best summed up by a saying of the times: "Carmel by the Sea, Pacific Grove by God... and Monterey by the smell." But in these uncertain times it was also "the smell of prosperity." The industry and its work force tolerated it; the City of Monterey objected to it; the Hotel Del Monte's Samuel F. B. Morse was infuriated by it. Yet, because the industry's continued survival—at least as it was structured—depended on it, the death-like stench of the reduction process should have been seen as a warning of impending consequences requiring effective resolution.

The canning process also changed significantly as a result of the production demands of World War I. The early "French Method" of frying in oil was completely replaced by mechanized steam cooking of sealed cans by workers that lived above the Cannery Row waterfront in the district called New Monterey. The industry's expansion also happened in an

(Continued on Page 47)

This early-1920s aerial view of Ocean View Avenue and its growing canyon of canneries prior to the construction of the large American Can Company can making plant on the open slopes above the Monterey Boat Works at China Point. G. E. Russell Aero Photo [2015-024-003]

Monterey's canneries were forced to locate outside the harbor on the rocky coastline along Ocean View Avenue. Underwater rocks and sea-mounts made it a treacherous unloading area for Monterey's fleet. Cable lines for steel buckets were rigged from cable dock towers high on the canneries, such as seen in this circa 1927 photo of Cal-Pac and Carmel Canning Co. canneries, unloading lighters safely offshore. [73-020-014]

A night's catch had to be unloaded from lampara lighters (barges) a bucket at a time up the cables to the cable docks at the canneries. The steel buckets held roughly 600 lbs. of fish. Lighters could hold up to 40 tons. [73-020-012]

(Continued from Page 45)

The bucket and cable off-loading system would soon change.   [73-020-013]

The "French frying" method would fade quickly after World War I.   [76-007-003]

American age before income tax, so the huge profits from the good times in the industry were often the windfall Steinbeck alludes to later in his introduction to his 1945 novel, *Cannery Row*, in which he muses that some canners were upset if unable to recover their entire investment each season. This was, of course, a stretch of the imagination, but not entirely without an actual basis.

Conditions in the canneries were at first archaic, to say the least, and unsafe under almost any assessment. Open gears, live steam, chain drives, and canvas belt-to-wheel drives proliferated an inventory of dangerous machinery and equipment in addition to the risks in the hand-cutting of the catch with knives and the inevitable nicks and accidents and infections associated with even expert cutters.

There were at first no controls on hours or shifts in the industry. Workers were called to the canneries by whistle, often before dawn, to pack the night's catch being unloaded by bucket and cable off Cannery Row. Work continued until the day's catch was canned — whatever time that took. A day's work could be six hours, or sixteen hours. The conditions prevailed decades before disability, medical plans, workmen's compensation insurance, child-care, or pensions. It would be the late 1930s before union activity would effectively change working conditions prevalent in the canneries and reduction plants of Ocean View Avenue. Until then, a look around would find a largely immigrant, multi-cultural work force, many of its workers struggling in or near poverty with cannery workers laboring under crude and arduous conditions in a seasonal industry whose owners and investors cast the dice of fate each season in which fortunes were made or lost on the strength of the sardine's seasonal return and the international market for the large Monterey pilchard.

Ocean View Avenue canning was a truly international pursuit, from its markets to its multi-ethnic workforce. This photo of the crew of the Japanese owned Bayside cannery is a typical record of the multi-national labor force in Monterey's burgeoning sardine canning industry.   [78-001-013]

ACTS OF GOD AND TRIALS BY FIRE

The powerful Pacific was to shake any complacency from its Monterey mariners with its periodic ravaging of the unprotected fleet; no breakwater would be constructed until the early thirties. The worst such storm destroyed 93 lampara boats on the Monterey Beach on Thanksgiving, 1919 — an especially heavy blow given the post-war recession in the fishing and canning industry. It would take another "natural" disaster to provide the protection the harbor needed.

The nearby petroleum storage tanks which Murray had ignored when purchasing the Tevis Estate were struck by lightning on September 14, 1924. The fire lasted two days before exploding into a river of flaming oil running into the sea. In its path were the canneries of California Fisheries and E.B. Gross — and the Tevis-Murray estate. The canneries were destroyed and the mansion and its massive windmill only narrowly escaped the same fate. The Associated Oil Company Pier — which loaded tankers bound for Richmond — was destroyed completely as the oil, blazing on the bay, drifted perilously toward Fisherman's Wharf... until the wind and tide changed!

Only two weeks later, on the night of September 28, the luxurious Hotel Del Monte burned to the ground for the second time. It would reopen, redesigned, the following May.

Fire would also call on Knut Hovden ... twice. The first major fire on August 12, 1921, destroyed the cannery in a fire that lasted two days fed by vats of sardine oil. Hovden's reconstruction included a larger and more modern plant. The second fire occurred October 5, 1924, gutting the reduction plant in a $20,000 inferno. But the King of Cannery Row

each time rebuilt, although at great difficulty in the recession-plagued early twenties.

Fisherman's Wharf and Booth were not to escape the call of fate. By the first of March, 1923, canneries had loaded the wharf with twenty thousand cases of sardines for shipment on the freighter "San Antonio." Without a breakwater yet to shield the harbor from unpredictable swells, the "San Antonio" lurched against the Wharf, damaging it and dumping 8,000 cases of still-to-be-loaded sardines into the bay.

Frank Booth was to be the victim of a similar fate on February 2, 1927, when 4,000 cases fell through the floors of his harbor cannery warehouse into the bay. The twenties had, indeed, "roared" in Monterey.

Hotel Del Monte in a Russell Aero Photo circa 1920.   [81-006-007]

Monterey's first Fire Chief, William "Billy" Parker, stands amid the ruins of the smouldering Hotel Del Monte, September 28, 1924—the second time the luxurious hotel had burned to the ground.   Lewis Josselyn [71-001-122]

48

On Thanksgiving Day, 1919, a devastating storm struck Monterey's exposed harbor. A protective breakwater would not be constructed until 1934. The storm struck the vulnerable fleet at anchor, destroying nearly one hundred lampara boats and lighters. This disaster came at an already poor time in the recession plagued industry's post World War I recovery.				Lewis Josselyn [71-001-311]

Storm damage to was not limited to the exposed fishing fleet. In a decade of disasters, the canneries of Ocean View Avenue paid dearly for their construction on the shoreline. This A. C. Heidrick photo shows the Carmel Canning Company deluged by huge storm waves on February 26, 1927.   [87-050-001]

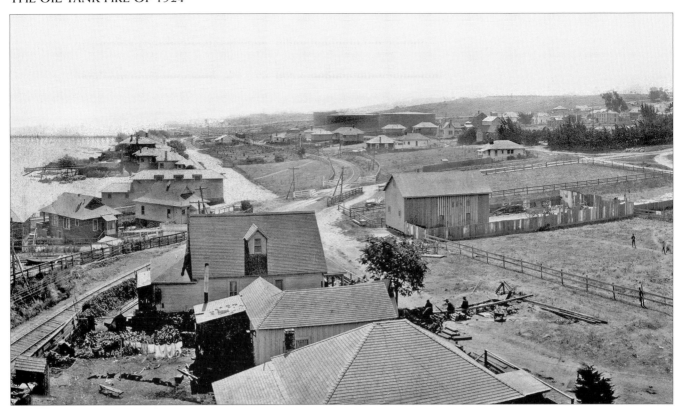

Crude Oil pumped from Coalinga (Coaling Station A), closer to Frenso than Monterey, was stored at the tank farm seen in the upper background of this photo from a rooftop looking over the elegant Tevis-Murray-Haldorn Estate. In the distant upper-left background, is the Associated Oil Company wharf that transferred oil to tankers bound for refining in Richmond, in the San Francisco Bay area. This is also the earliest known view of the fateful intersection where, in 1948, Edward F. Ricketts was struck by the evening Del Monte Express train that emerged from behind a huge warehouse built on the vacant, wedge-shaped lot at the center of the photo. Two early canneries on the far side of the ocean-front estate are obscured from this view, the Japanese-owned California Fisheries Company, and the Funston & Gross Packing Company.   *A.C. Heidrick circa 1920* [76-009-004]

The Coalinga Oil and Transportation Pier, later known as the Associated Oil Pier, filled tankers headed to Richmond and Martinez. This 1919 photo shows the Pacific Fleet at anchor at Monterey. The Monterey breakwater would eventually be built on its burned pilings.   *R. J. Arnold* [GL 76-044-003]

Above: September 14, 1924, lighting struck the petroleum storage tanks above the Associated Oil Company pier that stored crude oil from a pipeline originating in Coalinga. It burned uncontrolled for two days before exploding. Dan Freeman [82-029-033]
Right: The view down Ocean View Avenue toward the fire as firefighters, totally unequipped to fight an oil fire of such magnitude with only water, worked tirelessly to protect the Tevis-Murray Estate and its windmill. [87-019-0001]

On September 16th, 1924, the uncontrollable blaze resulted in an explosion of one of the tanks, spreading quickly to the others, killing two Presidio servicemen fighting the fire. A flaming river of crude oil roared down the hillside and through the Funston & Gross and California Fisheries canneries and onto the bay, literally setting it ablaze. The perilously close Tevis estate and its windmill narrowly escaped the inferno. Dan Freeman photo [85-011-073]

September 16, 1924, the flaming river of oil spread onto Monterey Bay and was being swept toward Fisherman's Wharf.   Dan Freeman [82-029-029]

The eerie inferno burning on Monterey Bay consumed the Coalinga Oil and Transportation Pier, a number of hapless boats, and was about to reach the pilings of Fisherman's Wharf when the wind and tide changed. In this photo, the Booth cannery at left, and the Wharf, watch the fire burn out in a near miss.

Dan Freeman [82-029-034]

A flaming river of oil to the sea followed the explosion of the petroleum tanks above the southeast end of Cannery Row. Ed Gross rebuilt; California Fisheries did not. *Lewis Josselyn [71-101-103]*

E.B. Gross watches local pharmacist and locksmith, Cecil Gretter, attempt to open Gross' cannery safe, one of the few recognizable remains after the fire that vaporized his Funston & Gross cannery and its neighbor, California Fisheries. *[85-011-001]*

The remains of the oil tank farm viewed from the former Funston & Gross cannery and the Japanese export California Fisheries Company. *Lewis Josselyn [71-001-101]*

53

METAMORPHOSIS

It was as if the whole of Monterey was caught up in a sudden, accelerated transformation. The sleepy, isolated pueblo of Spanish Monterey was suddenly all but gone except for the few adobes and other early Monterey architecture saved from demolition in the awakening of a new civic consciousness. A momentum established in the twenties would carry Monterey into the decade of the thirties, including its Great Depression, propelled by sardines!

Lingering memories of whaling along these shores, a Chinatown, and the graceful feluccas of its early Italian fishermen were quickly fading into the realities of boat yards, choruses of cannery whistles, and the steady growth of a fishing and canning industry upon which Monterey would become far too dependent. Where had the little town gone? The answer lay in sardines: a town and nearly its entire economy was becoming tied up in, serving, or prospering in the commerce of one of the world's greatest natural resources, Sardinops caerulea.

Reports by the Department of Fish & Game and alarms raised by fisheries biologists warned that the imminent depletion of the resource must be coming, but could not be proven. The boats and the fleet got bigger, the nets deeper, and the catches undiminished, so as long as long as the supply of sardines held out, those in the fishing and cannery industry effectively ridiculed and discredited their critics. Invention and investment became partners with work and pay. It was the convergence of technical advances and commercial opportunity that would doom the 11-inch fish that greased the gears of prosperity in a decade that first had to rise from the greatest depression

The graceful Italian feluccas that helped launch the stuttering Monterey fishing industry were soon only memories as motorized boats replaced them. [83-030-001]

in our nation's experience. The crushing economic devastation of the Great Depression only further sealed the fate of the sardines: a new mantra became "Fish or jobs?" They took the fish...and in the end, lost the fish and the jobs.

Alvarado Street, 1920, with its street-car tracks and establishments, including the Poppy—used in John Steinbeck's "Sweet Thursday"—and the Bay State Cafe of Mr. Maen Chang Wu, who in a few more years would build the Ocean View Hotel.   *R. J. Arnold photo [GL 89-033-272]*

The Boatworks of Pearson and Chochran, 1918, where many of the Monterey lampara boats were built.   A. C. Heidrick photo [82-040-001]

The Pacific Fleet calls on Monterey on August 31, 1919. Monterey is still without a protective breakwater.   A. C. Heidrick photo [79-104-003]

An industrial survey photo from the early 1920s shows the Hovden cannery crew in Monterey's primary industry.   [86-052-001]

Lighthouse Avenue, Pacific Grove, 1932, in a community rapidly emerging from its staid origins as a Methodist summer retreat. Both Ed Ricketts and John Steinbeck lived here into the 1930s.   Lewis Josselyn photo [71-001-263]

55

THE MEN, THE BOATS

Pietro Ferrante, Orazio Enea, Salvatore Russo, Constantine Balbo, Marco Lucido and Salvatore Lucido — men fated to come to Monterey in 1907 from Black Diamond (now Pittsburg) on the Sacramento River —set out in the "Crescent" and "Queen Esther" on a Monterey experiment with a Mediterranean net for a fish other men still had to learn to can.

Pietro Ferrante brought Sicilian fishermen from Booth's operation at Black Diamond on the Sacramento River (Pittsburg) to Monterey to use it. Thus began the Sicilian mastery of the Monterey fishing industry.
A. C. Heidrick photo [96-005-001]

Their success saw the romantic felucca's that once dotted the bay with lateen sails, yield to "Monterey Clippers" towing lighters of fish back to the harbor or anchor off Cannery Row to unload by bucket-and-cable.

The success of the lampara boat and its role in cannery supply seemed a near perfect match for the predominantly Sicilian immigrants that first manned, and then owned them. Their cost and that of the net was within the reach of many of the fishing families being established on the hill above the harbor. Several men and a great deal of hard work could produce a good, if frugal livelihood — even ownership of a good and lucky boat. But they had set in motion forces that would soon make the ever improving technology the master, not the servant, of the men who followed its call to the sea.

The insatiable appetites of Monterey's canneries and reduction plants now required a far more complex organization of the means of supply. Establishing the season price between canners and fishermen grew more complicated as the number of boats and owners multiplied into the 1920s. An effective strike for a price increase by the combined boat owners and fishermen in the 1927 season was to bring far-reaching consequences, again at the hands of technology. Hovden threatened to break the strike by bringing boats up from San Pedro, which as a tuna port brought into the sardine business by World War I, was far ahead of Monterey in vessel development.

On July 19, 1927 purse seiners "Admiral" and "Mariposa" cruised into Monterey Bay. The vessels were larger and swifter than anything Monterey's lampara fleet could have imagined. Their size, at over fifty feet in length, incorporated a protected wheel-house and cabin, large diesel engines, power winches for the huge purse seine (net), a revolving turntable aft on which the net was stacked for rapid redeployment and a hold capacity of thirty-five tons! It meant no more lighters to be towed, a range that opened up new fishing grounds, and an enormous net that closed at the bottom to securely entrap far greater amounts of sardines at a time than a canner's dream. A month later the strike was settled in a compromise, but Monterey had again been changed forever: the means by which the unconscious depletion of the Monterey sardine could be accomplished had arrived.

The introduction of the purse seiner brought with it a wave of controversy in the boat owners and fishermen's ranks.

A show-down of old friends led "Pete" Ferrante into retirement as Orazio Enea's demands for a "closed shop" organization of boat owners and fishermen heated up a tangled series of organizational attempts dating back to 1914. The resolution also had an interesting side effect. Won Yee, the squid baron of Monterey, had used the internal division of Sicilian boat owner groups for years to form a squid marketing monopoly in which the Sicilian rivalries insured the depressed price of squid, much to Yee's stoic benefit. Sicilian lampara technology, which had eliminated the Chinese from their own squid fishing industry, had made unwitting restitution.

The cost of entry into this new age of big boats and huge nets was, of course, astronomical by Monterey standards. A "half-ring" net, resembling the purse seine, was installed on most of the lampara boats as a stop-gap measure. Requiring little modification to the boats, it could capture nearly the same tonnage as the early purse seine — but still required the use of the accompanying lighter in which to put the catch. The purse seiner age had arrived amid resentment and controversy in the lampara entrenched industry at Monterey.

In an ironic twist, the purse seiner "Admiral" sank in January 1928, fortunately without loss of life, attempting to haul in an oversize catch. The first small Monterey-built purse seiner, the "Santa Lucia," joined the fleet the following season under contract to the E. B. Gross Cannery. Legislation in 1929 also established the Monterey sardine season between August 1 and February 15. Within the next few seasons the replacement of the lampara by half-rings was followed by new and even larger purse seines and seiners, setting the stage for an awesome new fishing capability centered around the new wolves of the sea.

Through the thirties the expansion of the Monterey sardine fleet and matching canning capacity would record annual tonnage landed at Monterey in excess of 200,000 tons per season in 1934-35, 1936-37, and 1939-40. The decade of the thirties was to be fraught with controversy and confrontation, almost entirely involved in the resolution of the quantities of fish the industry was to take, and what was then to be done with them. The agonizingly slow recovery from the Depression made reasoning even more difficult as the industry argued that its very survival rested on increased limits for reduction of whole fish.

Open reduction at sea by freighters converted to floating reduction plants resisted effective controls by operating beyond territorial limits until stopped by legislation in 1938. Deliveries to these "floaters" were made directly from purse seiners, whose nets were typically over a quarter of a mile long and extended to a depth of ten stories! Only time would reveal the awesome cost of this off-shore conspiracy.

Most of Monterey's Sicilian immigration was drawn predominantly from the fishing villages and islands around the capital city of Palermo.

Nino DiMaggio's "Caterina" at Booth's with lighters, a typical "Monterey Clipper" design utilized by the Sicilian lampara fishermen of the 1920s. Powered by a Hick's one cylinder, two-cycle engine, its unique bow design deflected waves; also famous as one of the most stable boat types ever built. [74-020-010]

Unloading a lighter (towed barge) of sardines at Booth's cannery in the Monterey harbor, the only cannery with dock-side off-loading. At Cannery Row it was done by an arduous cable and bucket process. [87-032-003]

Fishermen unload the Japanese lighter, S. Oyama, one bucket at time up to the unloading dock at Booth's harbor cannery. Booth's was the only cannery where boats could tie up directly next to the unloading facility. [74-020-001]

The "Admiral," one of the first two purse-seiners at Monterey, brought up from San Pedro by Hovden to break a 1927 lampara fisherman's strike. It was diesel powered, with a cabin, galley, bunks, a power winch, and boom for stacking the net on a revolving turn-table for immediate re-use. Anthropologist Dr. Linda Pitcher has determined it was built in 1915 in Tacoma, south Puget Sound. The 1930 season had 24 purse-seiners and 44 lampara boats with ring-nets. [74-020-033]

Lampara boats equipped to use the purse-seine still required lighters to put their catch in. When the larger "half-ringers" filled their holds to capacity, they poured fish onto the vessel's walkways making a "deck load" as Pete Cardinale's "Geraldine-Ann" at a Monterey harbor pier. Fishermen worked for "shares" of the catch rather than wages, accounting for the happy faces on this crew. [80-057-001]

Early purse seiner fleet at anchor at Monterey before a night's work with nets over a quarter mile long and ten stories deep. Chester Toombs [85-019-074]

Peak-season picture of the Monterey fishing fleet at anchor, often one hundred boats or more. Why isn't the fleet out fishing? The answer, of course, is that sardines were fished a night during the three weeks of darkened moon each month. They were found in the darkness by the fluorescent "green flash" caused by the turbulence of acre-sized schools of sardines feeding near the surface. Ray Ruppel photo [74-008-002]

During the week of the full moon each month of the season, the cotton nets were disassembled for repair and boiling out. Fred Harbick [73-006-015]

In an age before modern mono-filament nets, the maintenance of the huge cotton-cord purse-seine nets required regular, periodic cleaning in order to preserve the cotton fibers from damage by the oils and acids of the fish captured in them. Tan bark, often from Partington Ridge, Big Sur, was used for the tannin solution in which the nets were boiled to purge the damaging chemicals absorbed by the cotton. Nets then had to be skillfully reassembled by the crews for use as soon as the moon darkened and moonless nights helped spot the green flash of phosphorescence of sardine shoals.   *1947 Fred Harbick photo [89-030-089]*

MISCONCEPTION AND TECHNIQUE

Perhaps the two most frequently misunderstood factors in the saga of Monterey sardine history concern the fish themselves and the technique of their capture. The first misconception concerns the size of the Monterey sardine—or pilchard—which routinely reached eleven inches in length. This is obviously not its finger-sized Atlantic cousin still so popular, and in commercial supply by a number of nations still in the trade. The large size of the Monterey sardine and the weakness of a dependable domestic market made it a difficult food commodity to promote: American acceptance of canned fish of this type remained traditionally low except during ration demands of wartime. Peacetime overseas markets met stiff and systematically subsidized competition by Russian, Japanese, South American and North Sea industries.

A second, perhaps even more interesting misconception involves the fishing technique itself: it was conducted almost exclusively at night. In an age before sonar, locating vast but illusive schools of sardines required far more than fisherman's luck: the experience of the skipper was of the utmost importance. The trained eye and experience of a seasoned skipper and crew could spot the "green flash" of phosphorescence on the dark waters of moonless nights caused by the turbulence of millions of schooling fish.

Really skilled eyes distinguished between sardines and a disastrous catch of anchovy or horse mackerel. Anchovy could plug the smaller mesh of the "bag" of the huge net. Impossible to clear of anchovy at sea, and with huge effort, a plugged net had to be dragged back to the tannin tanks at the harbor and boiled of the oily acids that threatened to almost dissolve the cotton net. Monthly maintenance of the cotton-cord nets was crucial to their effectiveness and longevity. Seasoned experience was paramount to success.

"Making a set" with a net a quarter of a mile long, being deployed off a moving boat on the open sea in nearly total darkness (lights drew company and competition) required courage, skill and a level of teamwork difficult to envision. Although often referred to as "Italians," the men whose labor and skill dominated the Monterey fishing industry came from the coastal cities near Palermo, Sicily. Any Sicilian will be happy to explain the difference. (Refer to page 56)

The set began by dropping the skiff, attached to one end of the net, off the back of the purse seiner. The crewman in the skiff deployed a sea anchor, a parachute-like device that when submerged acted like a brake, allowing the purse seiner to pull away on its arc through the portion of the school of sardines selected by the skipper. However, crews constantly recalled the fate of the "Admiral": taking too much can sink you! The Seiner completed its encirclement of the catch to connect its end of the net to the skiff. Hundreds of large cork floats kept the net afloat. A cable running through rings at the bottom of the lead-weighted net was drawn in by winch to purse the net closed below the fish.

The boom and tackle lifted the net to the turntable as the power-winch drew in the pursed net until the last section of the net, the bag, drew alongside. Only then could the crew measure the catch to ensure that it met minimum size specifications for acceptance by Fish & Game inspectors at the canneries. This brings us to another major factor in the sardine supply: a catch of sardines with an average size too small to be accepted at Monterey was dumped at sea — usually killing nearly all of sardines taken in the set. This loss at sea, before the excesses in reduction of delivered fish, is inestimable.

A large dip-net resembling a horn of plenty, when tipped and emptied into the seiner's hold, transferred fish from the bag to boat. If the huge net contained more sardines than the capacity of the seiner's hold, it was common to pour excess fish onto the walkways and deck, which was referred to as a "deck load." For exceptionally large catches, sharing the extra fish unable to be carried was common among friendly boats.

In the late twenties the old cable-and-bucket method of off-loading fish to the canneries was augmented and then replaced, by a system of sturdy floating wooden pens called "hoppers," anchored safely out from Cannery Row's treacherous shoreline. The hoppers, introduced by Hovden in 1927, were connected by hard-hat divers to large flexible hoses to the underwater pipelines to the canneries. Each cannery employed massive turbine pumps to literally suck sardines ashore for processing. This major innovation solved the tremendous problem of quickly unloading large quantities of sardines from the increasing size and number of purse-seiners entering the Monterey sardine fleet.

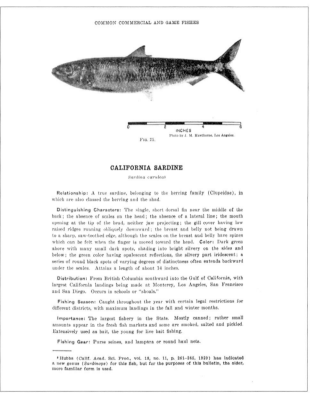

Detail from the Bureau of Commercial Fisheries, Fish Bulletin No.28: Handbook of Common Commercial and Game Fishes of California, by Lionel A. Walford, 1931.

- Monterey's sardines were up to 12" long
- They were caught at night, except the week of the full moon each month of the season
- Skippers found sardines in the darkness by the green phosphorescence on the surface of the sea caused by the turbulence of the feeding schools of fish
- In 1929, the annual sardine season was established from August 1st to February 15th
- An estimated billion sardines were taken from Monterey waters in an average season
- Two-thirds of the sardines landed at Monterey never saw a can at all! They were ground, pressed for their oil, and baked into fish meal and fertilizer

61

Crewmen dressed well as they set out for their seiners in the "skiff" that would anchor one end of the huge net when "set."　　Fred Harbick [73-006-023]

The skiff and its crewman would hold one end of the net with an underwater parachute device, known as a "sea anchor," as the seiner circled the catch to join the ends of the nets at the skiff, purse the net closed at the bottom, and winch it in—stacking it on the seiner's revolving turntable.　　[73-040-001]

Work with the heavy, wet net in the darkness on a rocking boat was dangerous and exhausting work. The net is stacked on the turntable, which can then be rotated for redeployment and the "set" process is ready to begin all over again.   *George Robinson photo* [81-021-014]

When the "bag" of the net is finally drawn up next to the seiner, the fish are held for brailing into the hold.   [77-019-004]

The dip net on Skipper Tom Cardinalli's "City of Monterey" is a classic example of what was often referred to as "the horn of plenty"—and another classic reminder of the size of the Monterey sardine.   George Robinson photo.   [81-021-018]

By dawn, the fleet is lined up at the cannery hoppers along Cannery Row to unload the night's catch.   William L. Morgan photo [80-045-008]

John Steinbeck aptly describes purse-seiners like Skipper John Russo's "Star of Monterey" waddling into the Bay to off-load at the cannery hoppers. Riding this low meant a good catch and that meant a good pay day for crewmen that worked for shares, not by the hour. [80-045-003]

The old cable and bucket off-loading system was impossible to manage with the large size and catches of the purse seiners introduced in the late 1920s. Knut Hovden devised the slope-sided floating pens into which the seiner catch was brailed and then sucked by pump to the cannery. [79-111-003]

Occasionally catches exceeded the hold-capacity of the seiner and fish were shared with other friendly boats or those contracted to the same cannery. Such a transfer is shown here with a Japanese crew guiding the "horn of plenty" to their hold. Albert Campbell photo circa 1940 [77-009-008]

CHANGING FORTUNES

The end of World War I, and its ensuing recession, saw a scramble for survival by the sardine factories along Cannery Row. The addition of new canneries contributed to the constantly changing face of the street as well.

Frank Raiter's San Xavier cannery opened at the north end of the Murray estate in 1917; Bernard Senderman, former partner in Pacific Fish Company, preferred retirement to further risk at his newly completed cannery, selling to local investors who opened it as Carmel Canning Company in January, 1920; the Japanese venture at Great Western Sardine Company becomes Sea Pride Packers; Pacific Fish Company sold to California Packing Corporation (Del Monte) in March, 1926; the American Can Company began construction on a huge can making plant across the Pacific Grove line in July, 1926; the San Carlos Cannery, opened by Angelo Lucido in 1927, was owned by boat owners and fishermen; Bayside Fish and Flour became Cypress Canning Company briefly in 1927 before becoming Ed David's Del Mar Canning Company; Old Custom House Packing Corporation, formed in April, 1929, joined at the shoulders with Carmel Canning at Hoffman Avenue and Ocean View Avenue.

What they all had in common was the processing of fish, and without great variation their geometry and layout were uncannily similar: the off-loading, weighing, cutting, packing, and cooking of the sardines were conducted on the ocean-side of the street. Straddling Ocean View Avenue to connect production to the cannery's warehouses were the crossovers—or bridges—by which canned sardines were transported across the street for storage, labeling and shipment from the Southern Pacific tracks at their back doors.

Each of the steps in processing was also roughly the same; the efficiency of the process often determined its fate.

Monterey sardines were typically "French fried" in peanut oil prior to 1911, when steam cooking was introduced. By the end of World War I, the industry was mechanized to produce sardines pre-cooked in steam, mechanically sealed in their cans, and pressure cooked in them to complete the process. This was nothing less than a revolution in industrial time. That did not mean that the fish would always be there to be cooked in their cans or turned into fish meal. Times change.

Changing fortunes in a later time: the Æneas Sardine Products Company being built in 1945, just before the crash. George Seideneck [72-012-049]

The San Carlos Cannery was initially owned by boat owners and fishermen, headed by of Angelo Lucido. One of the barons of Cannery Row, Lucido sponsored many immigrating countrymen and utilized their talent and labor to become a major force in the industry.　　　*A. C. Heidrick [81-025-002]*

ABOUT THE ABALONE

A colorful German restaurateur, Pop Ernest Doelter, operated a restaurant on Alvarado Street in Monterey. His specialty was "abalone steak" cut from abalone, a large mollusk almost unknown and unrecognized by most American tastes, though highly regarded by Oriental cultures.

His innate promotional skills established abalone as a new and fashionable delicacy, especially after his spectacular success at the Panama Pacific Exposition in San Francisco in 1915, where he introduced the ubiquitous Oriental delicacy to the "Western" world as abalone steak.

In 1919, he moved his restaurant from downtown Monterey to the entrance to Fisherman's Wharf and continued to champion his signature specialty. Problems with the source of his good fortune began in 1915 when the Japanese were prohibited by law from canning and exporting abalone.

Difficulties plagued the industry over the years but Pop's fortunes took a definite turn for the worse years later when, in 1932, the Japanese abalone diving operation at Point

Pop Ernest, "Father of the abalone steak."   Rey Ruppel [82-031-007]

"Pop" Ernest's at the Fisherman's Wharf   [74-006-013]

Lobos—the focal source of supply—ceased operation. The former Chinese cove, Portuguese whaler's outpost, and finally the industrious Japanese abalone diving industry and cannery, all faded into obscurity as the point became a state park. Pop Ernest's died in 1934, having introduced the mollusk to the palates of generations willing now to pay a ransom for what was then merely an unusual, formerly Oriental, delicacy. Pop Ernest's appears in interior restaurant scenes with Barbara Stanwyk in R.K.O.'s "Clash By Night" filmed in 1951. His sons continued operating the restaurant until 1952.

Abalone, once dried or canned for export at Point Lobos, became a signature Monterey seafood—"Abalone Steak"—at "Pop Ernest's."   [83-040-01]

Booth's Cannery and wharf above and the angled Pop Ernest's restaurant at the entrance to Fisherman's Wharf in 1938.   Ted McKay [83-006-005]

Abalone shell mounds like this, evidence of an abundance until the mid-1930s, were fairly common around the peninsula. Lewis Josselyn   [71-001-137]

Boilermen brought the canneries to life before dawn, firing the huge boilers that would cook the fish and—prior to electrification—provided power to gear drives, link-chain and belt-and-pulley drive equipment throughout the cannery. It was the boilerman who routinely whistled cannery workers to begin their day's toil at the packing tables and canning equipment. Each cannery had its own distinct whistle pitch and blast pattern to call its workers to the lines in an age before telephones in the working class home.

Fish unloaded at the hoppers were pumped ashore by the large turbines in the cannery's pump-house. The fish were then moved by escalator high up into the canneries for California Department of Fish & Game inspection and weighing. Gravity and hydraulic flows were used to move the processing of the fish along wherever possible.

Fish cutting traditionally done manually by Chinese and Japanese and Spanish workers became cheaper and less specialized by nationality after the introduction of machine cutters. Slotted conveyors in which the sardines were placed were drawn under spinning blades that cut off the heads and tails and automatically eviscerated the fish.

The next stop on the trip to the can was at the packing tables, another conveyor system that moved the cut and prepared fish down a packing line. The famous one-pound oval can — the trademark of Monterey's sardine packing industry — was a curious holdover from the industry's salmon packing origins. Frank Booth, in his early sardine canning experiments, found that five or six Monterey pilchards fit neatly into the oval can. The salmon had passed into the lore of Monterey's

early fish packing years, but left this unique memento of its one-time precedence: it was for this can that the young Knut Hovden invented the first machine solderer-sealer for Frank Booth.

Cans for the packing lines were often fed down track-like chutes from the floors above to await mating with lids at the sealing machines. Packed cans, depending on the cannery process, might be pre-cooked open before being inverted by machines designed to drain them before sealing. The last step on the way to the sealing machines was usually the addition of tomato sauce, mustard sauce, olive oil or other special seasonings.

Sealed cans of sardines filled large rolling steel retort baskets, which were then loaded into huge retorts (pressure cookers) to cook at 15 pounds pressure for about an hour and a half. "The Chef was a boilerman in overalls, watching and regulating steam pressure and temperatures in the retorts.

Cooling rooms were often provided for the hot cans, often waiting overnight in their retort baskets before they could be sent across the street on the cross-over conveyors to be labeled and fed to "can catchers" for casing-up and storage in the warehouses. Each warehouse had box makers who fabricated the cases used by the men catching and casing up the cans.

Often cans were cased for storage unlabeled, waiting for the particular order or client brand for which they would be labeled. Finally they were loaded into freight cars for the trip down the Southern Pacific tracks to Castroville and to the main line and the world.

Thrity-six "American women" at the three double-packing tables at Hovden's. Typical era photo and promotional commentary of the early Century.
A. C. Hiedrick [2002-049-001]

NO DIVERS, NO ROW

You will recall that in the early years the Lampara boats towed their lighters to the bucket cables extending from each cannery into the bay. The new purse-seiners required a totally different system to unload huge catches from their holds. Hovden struck upon a system of stout floating wooden pens, called hoppers, into which the seiners could brail their catches directly from their holds. The hoppers were connected to large, flexible rubber hoses to pipelines on the bottom of the bay to the canneries. Huge electric turbine pumps literally sucked sardines ashore into the Row's canneries. The compression of the fish though the pipes served to de-scale them as an added bonus to processing of the silver tide.

The ability of Cannery Row to achieve its incredible success in matching the delivery of often over 200,000 tons of fish per season with their processing into canned fish and by-products lies with the courage and skill of its cannery divers. In dive gear sometimes weighing over 150 pounds, they were responsible for anchoring the hoppers, connecting them to the thick rubber hoses and attaching them to hundreds of yards of 12″ iron pipe assembled underwater in 12 foot bolted-flange sections—in poor to zero visibility, tidal surges, and tons of shifting pipe.

The success of the world-famous Monterey sardine industry depended on the courage and skill of cannery divers. Any interruption in the flow of sardines from the floating hoppers and underwater pipelines was disastrous, usually requiring the shutdown of the entire cannery until it could be restored. Nor, could a season even begin without the installation, repair, replacement, realignment and maintenance of the hoppers and pipelines torn, twisted and damaged by the previous season's winter storms.

"Indispensable" describes the role of the cannery divers whose dangerous underwater work enabled the ability of the canneries of the Old Row to operate a full six month season each year. Monterey could never have become "The Sardine Capital of the World" without their heroic underwater exploits. Divers were: Oscar Lager, Eddie Bushnell, Henry Porter, Al Annand, Pete Constanti, Mitch Constanti, Larry Johnstone Tom Pierce, George Fraley, and Ralph Nonella. Two cannery divers, Henry Porter and Tom Pierce, died at their dangerous work under the waves of Monterey Bay. Dive tenders were: Andy Skov, Chet Bushnell, Dick McFadden, George Fraley, Ted Duffy, Danny Toms, Manuel Garcia, John Poskus, Ray Overton, and Ralph Nonella.

In 2009, the Cannery Row Foundation dedicated a memorial on the shoreline of San Carlos Beach Park to the skill and courage of Cannery Row's divers and tenders.

The early canning process began with bringing the fish ashore by cable and bucket.
A. C. Heidrick [2002-049-002]

Floating wooden hoppers replaced the cable and bucket off-loading system. The new increase in capacity to the canneries depended, however, on expert underwater hard-hat divers to anchor them, connect their pipes to the canneries, and maintain them through each season.
Donn Clickard [81-011-030]

Dive tender, Andy Skov, prepares Eddie Bushnell for a dive.
Photo courtesy George and Sylvia Fraley [2003-070-001]

71

Large concrete waterline bunkers at each cannery, called "pump houses," enclosed the huge turbine pumps that literally sucked fish ashore from the hoppers to the fish-ladders like this at Cal-Pac that carried them up to the top of the canneries to the scale house for weighing and then begin their gravity-driven process to the cutting machines, packing lines, cooking retorts—and the grinders and kilns of the reduction plants. George Robinson [81-021-022]

Canneries had a variety of scales to weigh the incoming boatloads of fish. A standard scale is shown here with a fisherman checking weights. [86-083-001]

At some canneries, fish inspection could be combined with scales that weighed the incoming catch on the fish conveyor.   *Rey Ruppel* [80-045-005]

The cutting machines utilized less skilled, and less expensive labor to cut fish for the packing tables.   Fred W. Harbick [72-020-004]

Expert, piecework hand cutting was eventually replaced by short conveyors with "slots" in which the fish were laid to be drawn under spinning blades that cut and automatically eviscerated the fish. Marilyn Monroe's first co-starring role was as a fish cutter on a machine like this in RKO's 1952 classic love triangle, "Clash By Night." There were lines of these machines in each cannery like these at Cal-Pac.   George Robinson [81-021-027]

One-pound "talls" were also often packed in parallel lines with those packing the 15 oz. "One Pound Ovals." *Fred Harbick [73-006-007]*

Can chutes from the upstairs can room, fed by cross-overs from warehouses, deliver one-pound oval cans down to these packing lines.
Donn I. Clickard [81-041-011]

Packing a world-famous trademark of Cannery Row—the one pound oval—at California Packing ("Cal-Pac") Plant 101. This was the same salmon can for which Knut Hovden invented the sealing machine, enabling the explosive expansion of the Monterey sardine industry. George Robinson [81-021-029]

At the end of the line was a skilled "re-packer" to fill oddly packed cans or repack spilled ones prior to sealing.   George Robinson [81-021-031]

Good mechanics were always in demand to keep the high-speed sealing machines functioning properly. Breakdowns were an expensive nemesis to the orderly and profitable flow of fish through the canneries.   George Robinson photo [81-021-030]

"Retort baskets," filled with sealed sardine cans to be pressure cooked at West-Gate Sun Harbor (formerly Del Mar)   Donn I. Clickard [81-041-009]

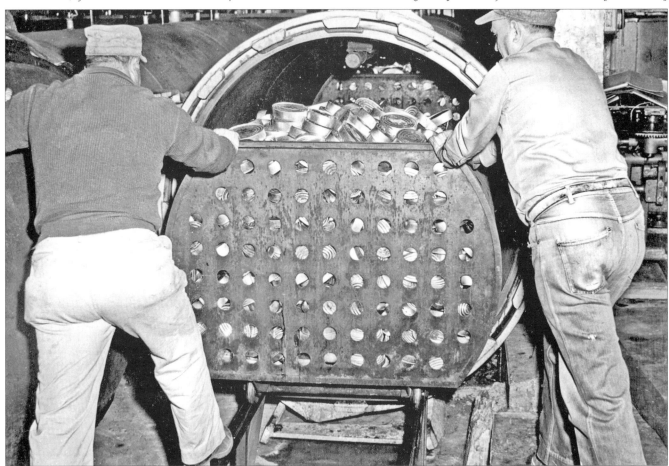

Filled retort baskets were rolled into horizontal pressure cookers called "retorts" and cooked by steam pressure.   [74-012-009]

"The Chef" in the sardine cooking process was in reality a boilerman who carefully monitored temperature and steam pressure gauges as the sardines, often packed in tomato or mustard sauce, cooked in their cans.

George Robinson photo [81-021-033]

Each cannery had a reduction plant which ground tons of edible fish into pulp called "cake," pressed and centrifuged it for its oil, then baked the mash into fish meal in kilns (above). Large plants had several of these rotary kilns, responsible for the horrendous odor of the process.   George Robinson [81-021-034]

The post-war era after World War I posed problems old and new. Without wartime demand, and the resumption of the Atlantic sardine fishery, Monterey's foreign markets for sardines declined toward their pre-war status, as did the domestic market. Unfavorable tariffs simply compounded perhaps the biggest problem: canner's speculation had resulted in warehouses full of sardines. Something to prop-up the industry was urgently needed as canneries sold, closed or went bankrupt.

Reduction and its huge profits on minimal investment and labor costs could no longer be ignored as a major part of the canning industry. The industry entered the 1920s with an ever-increasing pressure for legislation to permit larger scale reduction and by-product use of the catch. Warnings by the state's Department of Fish and Game specialists were pitted against industry survival: reduction profits would subsidize the depressed canning industry. The decade of the twenties was to establish this irreversible direction of the industry to profit at the uncertain expense of the fishery. Besides, as Hovden would state, "The sardine supply could not be exterminated," at a time when certain proof could not be produced to the contrary. The decade of the thirties would put tremendous industry pressure on California politics and challenges to limit regulation of the industry's plunge into reduction.

The reduction process itself was relatively simple, requiring modest investment and labor to operate. It did recover and make nearly complete use of vast amounts of fish processing waste, but it was also to blame for the stomach wrenching smell incorrectly blamed on canning of sardines. It was an impetus that irrevocably pointed the industry toward suicide. From early on, grinding of offal (the fish heads, tails and entrails) from the canning process was augmented by the diversion of increasing tonnage of whole, otherwise edible fish. The industry's increasingly powerful legislative lobby saw these otherwise edible sardines ground into pulp before being squeezed and centrifuged of liquid content. The remaining pulp, or "cake," was baked in rotary gas-fired kilns turning it into fish meal. The liquid pressed and centrifuged from the pulp was reduced by further cooking to a heavy consistency that sold as a poultry feed additive or was added back into the manufacture of "whole" meal fertilizer. It was not the canning of sardines, rather it was this "reduction" process, that resulted in Monterey's dubious fame for its famously fouled air.

Because the manufacture of fish meal and fertilizer was far simpler and more profitable than sardine canning, the packing of sardines ultimately became a sideline for the large scale reduction and by-product process: Monterey's canning industry had become a fish meal and fertilizer industry.

80

Can-catching and casing-up of cooked cans, box making, labeling and storage were the realm of the warehouse.   Fred Harbick [73-006-018]

In fishmeal warehouses, meal blown from the cannery was sacked and stored until loaded in boxcars or trucked to ships.   Fred Harbick [73-006-019]

The early "floater" in this William L. Morgan photo may be the "Brookdale"—first floating reduction plant in a fleet of reduction ships to operate off the California Coast in the 1930s. Their dramatic impact on the volume of sardines already diverted to fishmeal and fertilizer helped tip the balance of the survival of the Monterey sardine. It appears that too many mature sardines were taken to sustain reproduction levels and size of the fish. [89-072-011]

Warnings against the potential depletion of the sardine began in the early 1920s, before the wholesale reduction of sardines—the grinding, pressing, and baking of sardines into fish meal and fertilizer—came to account for the vast majority of fish tonnage landed and processed not only in Monterey, but on the entire West Coast in the 1930s. The first official biological warning of the possibility of depletion came in 1921 and was met with apathy and disregard. This warning came at time before the enormous volume of fish delivered directly for reduction to the floaters off the coast in the decade of the 1930s as shown in the detail from Table 8, on page 109.

The Great Depression made partners of business and labor to exploit the fishery on the unlikely prospect, in their view, that real damage could be done to the apparently limitless scale of the sardine stock.

Max M. Shaeffer's aggressive early leadership into land-based reduction as a discreet industry operating in parallel with canning fish, was mirrored in the 1930s by Stanley Hiller of Santa Cruz, who would lead the industry into avoiding state limits on reduction by processing unlimited amounts of sardines delivered to floaters directly by purse seiners beyond California's 3-mile legal jurisdiction. Hiller was already a major supplier of reduction equipment to canneries on shore and took a major role in fitting out freighters for use as sea-going reduction plants.

The Great Depression was still a dominant force in the pressure to keep the canneries operating and employment at maximum possible levels—even if such policies threatened the sardine supply. The addition of the fleet of unrestricted floaters to the relaxed limits for on-shore reduction facilities had consequences that were projected by fisheries biologists. With a sustainable yield of between 250,000 to 300,00 tons per season estimated by fisheries biologists, the annual take by the industry was two to three times as much. The resulting loss of such a volume of mature sardine breeding stock had a highly dramatic effect on reproduction in the succeeding seasons.

It is now widely agreed that the pressure on the biomass due to the addition of the floaters to the already excessive diversion of fish into reduction by on-shore plants was a blow from which the sardine stock never recovered.

Reproduction levels faltered in the following years, masked in part by the increasing efficiency of the new purse seine technology. In spite of factoring in temperature changes, currents, and other effects on the fishery, the failure to have reserved a critical level of mature breeding stock that could survive those pressures was an error once committed could not be reversed.

The failure of the spawning seasons of 1949 and 1950 are blamed for the final collapse of the fishery—a species "crash" being repeated all over the globe at this very moment.

TABLE 8
SEASONAL LANDINGS IN TONS
Sardines

Season*	Reduction ships	San Francisco area	Monterey area	Los Angeles area	San Diego area	Total tons
1916–17	----	----	7,710	17,380	2,440	27,530
1917–18	----	70	23,810	41,340	7,360	72,580
1918–19	----	450	35,750	32,530	6,810	75,540
1919–20	----	1,000	43,040	16,580	6,410	67,030
1920–21	----	230	24,960	11,740	1,520	38,450
1921–22	----	80	16,290	19,220	910	36,500
1922–23	----	110	29,210	33,170	2,620	65,110
1923–24	----	190	45,920	35,040	2,780	83,930
1924–25	----	560	67,310	96,330	8,820	173,020
1925–26	----	560	69,010	61,990	5,710	137,270
1926–27	----	3,520	81,860	64,720	2,110	152,210
1927–28	----	16,690	98,020	67,900	4,650	187,260
1928–29	----	13,520	120,290	119,250	1,420	254,480
1929–30	----	21,960	160,050	140,540	2,620	325,170
1930–31	10,960	25,970	109,620	38,490	80	185,120
1931–32	31,040	21,607	69,078	42,656	264	164,645
1932–33	58,790	18,634	89,599	83,605	62	250,690
1933–34	67,820	36,336	152,480	125,047	1,746	383,429
1934–35	112,040	68,477	230,854	178,818	4,865	595,054
1935–36	150,830	76,147	184,470	138,400	10,651	560,498
1936–37	235,610	141,099	206,706	138,115	4,594	726,124
1937–38	67,580	133,718	104,936	109,947	383	416,564
1938–39	43,890	201,200	180,994	146,403	2,800	575,287
1939–40	----	212,453	227,874	96,827	112	537,266
1940–41	----	118,092	165,698	175,592	1,202	460,584

Detail from the Department of Fish and Game, Fish Bulletin No. 149: The California Marine Fish Catch for 1968 and Historical Review 1916-1968, by Richard F. G. Heimann and John G. Carlisle, Jr., 1970. The full table can be found on page 109.

It is not just a little ironic that the sardines are back. It is known their appearance along the West Coast is a cyclical phenomenon—proven from scale counts in the ocean sediment indicating numbers of fish perhaps twice as large as their presence during the rise and fall of old Cannery Row. A number of converging factors sped their disappearance in the last century. Over fishing, reduction, as well as ocean temperature fluctuations and current changes affected the distribution and reproduction rates for the species. The "even so" statement still holds, however, that we did irreparable damage to our own livelihoods and lifetimes in the conduct of the fishing and canning industry at Monterey. The carelessness, greed, indifference and arrogance of our record here in the management of an incredible natural resource that could have continued for many more generations is one the world has yet to learn. Monterey, in the 1930s and 1040s, had the opportunity to control its own destiny. Instead, politics permitted profit over the intelligent conservation of the resource—and the question of "fish or jobs?" was answered with "jobs." The result was the loss of the fish... and the jobs. This is an ecological equation that demands attention and consideration in virtually every sustainable resource management situation around the globe.

It was economics—but especially hardships of The Great Depression—that created a willing collaboration between business and labor and government to subordinate the survival of the fishery to their own. The demand for fish meal and fertilizer as California agriculture expanded, and the off-shore floater reduction excesses of the 1930s ultimately spelled the early end of the Monterey sardine industry. It was simply a matter of time.

Loading a coastal freighter, the alternative to meal by rail.   [97-031-005]

With the vast majority of industrial production done on the ocean-side of Ocean View Avenue, the completed products were moved to the warehouse side by overhead "cross-overs" that enclosed conveyors and pipelines for fish oil. Some also enclosed large pipes through which fish meal was blown across the street to warehouses for grinding and sacking prior to shipment by rail from the rear of the canneries.　*Ted McKay photo [84-096-001]*

Ocean View Avenue "in-season" in the late 1930s. The cross-over proclaiming the massive Del Mar Cannery connects to its huge warehouse on the up-hill side of the Street. The luxury hotel now on the Del Mar plant site is the last hotel to be constructed within Monterey City limits.　*[72-124-001]*

A look at a typical warehouse crew on the Row in 1936--this one at the Hovden boxcar loading dock..   Courtesy Charles Nonella [86-061-001]

This Miles Midloch photo captures the feeling and spirit of its workers that the genius of John Steinbeck translated into "Cannery Row."   [81-051-002]

As the corrugated tin, plank, and stucco canyon of canneries that lined Ocean View Avenue grew in number and size, the cross-overs (covered conveyor and pipeline bridges) that vaulted the street also grew to transport supplies to the canning side of the street from the warehouse side. Those same bridges returned finished cans of sardines, oil—and in some cases, fish meal blown through pipes from reduction plants in the canneries on the ocean side of the street—back to their warehouses on the other.

Over the years there were a total of sixteen such cross-overs, or bridges, that combined to provide Cannery Row with its world-famous architectural feature, one that is employed in its contemporary commercial development.

Of the sixteen original cross-overs, two remain into the present-day life of Cannery Row. The oldest is the Monterey Canning Company crossover, serving its World War I era cannery built by Scotsmen A. M. Allan and George Harper in 1918. That cross-over has been adapted to become a pedestrian bridge over the street.

The other original of the sixteen bridges is that of the ÆNEAS PACKING COMPANY, a late entry into the industry in 1945, just before the crash of the fishery. It is, at this time, unserviceable but restored and maintained as an authentic icon of the industry that made Monterey famous and forever linked to the rise and demise of the sardine. And now for a look a the street of sixteen bridges.

Cannery worker, Hank Damewood, in the icon Cannery Row photo by George Seideneck, 1945. Like cannery worker Harold Otis Bicknell, the model for John Steinbeck's Mack of "Mack and the boys," Hank Damewood never anticipated his accidental role in Cannery Row history. [72-012-053]

Monterey Harbor Wharf #2, the fleet at Fisherman's Wharf, the F. E. Booth cannery, and the Presidio of Monterey at "Lighthouse Curve." [83-006-018]

John Steinbeck describes Cannery Row as the area between the harbor breakwater and the boat yard at China Point.   *Ted McKay* [83-006-025]

The mid-Row canneries of the San Xavier Packing Company, California Packing Corporation ("Cal-Pac") Plant 101, Carmel Canning Company, and Custom House Packing crowd the rocky shoreline for position. The Ocean View Hotel at McAbee Beach provides a rare ocean view from Ocean View Avenue before the street is walled-in again by Monterey Canning and the Del Mar canneries in this late 1930s Ted McKay photo.   [84-096-001]

At the far left, the cross-overs for Cal-Pac, Carmel Canning, and Custom House canneries vault Ocean View Avenue. The aging Ocean View Hotel peers out over McAbee Beach. Monterey Canning, Del Mar, Sea Pride, and the Hovden canneries complete this view of the Old Row.   Ted McKay [84-096-001]

This particular photograph is referred to as "The Neighborhood" for, in it, almost the entire book "Cannery Row" occurs. For a detailed historical and literary map and index of its sites and significance see the Cannery Row Map and Index on Pages 118-121. Ted McKay [83-006-062]

The American Can Company plant, Pacific Grove, on the upper part of the original Chinese settlement. Built in the mid-1920s, it rose to monopolize the can trade on the Row. Ted McKay [83-006-024]

The Nearly three-quarters of a mile from the Monterey harbor breakwater (now the Boatworks and Monterey Coast Guard Pier) to the American Can Company can plant (now the American Tin Cannery) lives on in relative historical obscurity. Real historical consciousness is, however, finally beginning to express itself on a world famous street still without any significant informational markers or signage to indicate and convey the factual identity and role of sites and remaining structures of historical and Steinbeck literary importance.

Keeping these photographic images in your mind and, with the aid of your imagination, it is still possible to see old Ocean View Avenue as it was and appreciate its stark and severe working conditions—and the haunts of Doc, and Mack and the boys in John Steinbeck's "Cannery Row." You will find Steinbeck wrote little fiction and much about real people and places here.

JOHN STEINBECK'S "CANNERY ROW"

ED RICKETTS' OLD OCEAN VIEW AVENUE

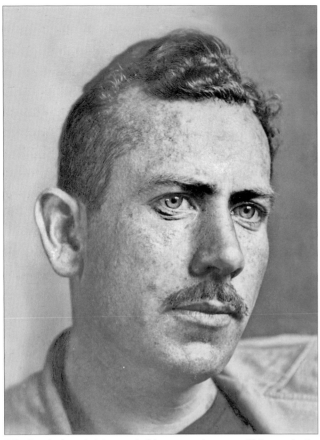

John Steinbeck made Monterey's fish canning district world-famous by his "fictional" accounts of its real inhabitants, alluding to its history only as color and background for the settings and scenes of their exploits. The photo above is of Steinbeck at 41 years of age. [2005-003-001]

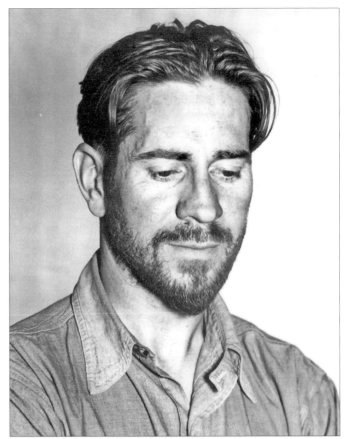

Marine biologist, Ed Ricketts, became John Steinbeck's closest friend, mentor and inspiration—and a number of his fictional literary characters. These roles did, however, obscure his major professional accomplishments as the pioneering leader of Ecology. Bryant Fitch photo [97-116-001]

John Steinbeck was born in 1902 into a middle-class family in Salinas, California, an agricultural center on the Southern Pacific rail-line. His mother, Olive, a former Big Sur school teacher kept a tight rein on her son and imbued John and three sisters with the importance of an education. John's talent for writing showed itself in wry and fanciful contributions to his Salinas High School year book.

John attended Stanford University, but intermittently, with little motivation or real intent to graduate. Rather John was determined to becoming a writer, with little interest in other scholastic pursuits. In the summer of 1923, John and his sister Mary attended a summer course on basic marine biology at Stanford University's Hopkins Marine Station on the Pacific Grove shoreline near the city limit with Monterey. That experience with science and the sea stuck a chord that would resonate throughout his life, particularly after meeting marine biologist Ed Ricketts. Ricketts was, in fact in and around Hopkins as he was establishing his marine biological supply house in 1923, but there is no evidence they ever met there. An introduction would wait until 1930 when he was introduced to Ed Ricketts at the home of Jack and Sasha Calvin, Ed's co-author of their inter-tidal handbook, "Between Pacific Tides." It would be 1939 before it was finally published, with pressure by Steinbeck on Stanford University Press by their famous non-alumnus.

John was Ed's almost constant companion from 1930 until 1935, when "Tortilla Flat" enabled Carol Steinbeck to choose a new home of their own near Los Gatos. John's decade of the 1930's in Ed's company provided him the inspiration and model for six major characters in his most prolific, and some say, finest literary output of his career. Ed's lab on Cannery Row anchored their friendship.

Edward Flanders Robb Ricketts was born on May 14, 1897 in Chicago. After service in late WWI, he attended University of Chicago intermittently for two years as part of an astute group of students under early academic ecologist Professor Clyde Warder Alee. His room-mate and others in his circle expounded on the biological diversity afforded by Stanford's Hopkins Marine Station in California.

In 1923, Ed left Chicago and traveled west to Pacific Grove to open a biological supply business with his Chicago room-mate, Albert Galigher. They named it Pacific Biological Laboratories, located on Fountain Avenue, a short distance uphill from the community beach at Lovers Point and fresh sea water for specimens.

The partners diligently built and expanded their client list of high schools, colleges and medical schools all over the country to which they shipped west coast specimens of all sorts, from marine invertebrates to monarch butterflies from Pacific Grove, to rattlesnakes from the sand dunes of Seaside. Ed specialized in the specimens, and Galigher in the microscope slides facet of the business. It was not long, however, before Ed bought out Galigher who moved his slide business to Berkeley.

Business grew, as did Ed's family of a son and two daughters. In the late 1920s, things did get complicated when Ed's landlords on Fountain Avenue gave him notice that the building he occupied was to be demolished. So began a search for a replacement location for Pacific Biological Laboratories. Until only recently the details of how the first lab relocated from downtown Pacific Grove to Ocean View Avenue in Monterey was shrouded by the clouds of history. Fortunately, curiosity and determination in an extraordinary quest to understand how 740 Ocean View Avenue became the new lab site was undertaken by a descendant of a troubled partnership of immigrant Spanish families.

The first Pacific Biological Laboratories was located in downtown Pacific Grove uphill from Central Avenue on Fountain Avenue, at the window and door in the first facade-front building in the far right of this only known photo of the site of this famous landmark with its alley now officially "Ricketts Row." [C.B. Clark 89-23]

The second location of Pacific Biological Laboratories was at 470 Ocean View Avenue behind the fence on the left. Across the street is a very rare glimpse at the Lone Star Cafe of Flora Wood which Steinbeck turns into the Bear Flag Restaurant in "Cannery Row." A few years after his death in 1948, the lab became a private men's club which, in effect, saved it from demolition. The men's club sold it to the City of Monterey in 1993 to keep it a Monterey historical treasure, open periodically for tours. [81-104-0001]

This is a rarest of photos of 740 Ocean View Avenue to date. [85-082-0002]

LA ESPERANZA FISH PACKING COMPANY

In late 1916, Joseph and Vincent Rodriguez decided to begin a sardine packing operation at 740 Ocean View Avenue on "Cannery Row" in New Monterey–which they rented and then purchased. Though not related, both men immigrated from the village of Sada in the Galacia region of Spain to San Francisco. Joseph was a fisherman and Vincent a shoemaker. With two other Spanish financial partners they purchased the property as a group and began the fish packing business.

The process of packing of sardines differed substantially from canning sardines underway along the street. The old-world method of preserving sardines involved soaking them in brine tanks, layering them in shallow wooden barrels and then pressing them for a several weeks. It is said the dried product resembled freeze-dried sardines, but its principal markets were overseas.

"La Esperanza"–meaning "The Hope"–failed its namesake. The first season's production was shipped by train to the east coast and vanished. Joseph Rodriguez traveled east by train attempting to find it. This kind of theft was by no means a rare occurrence in the railroads of the time and Joseph–unsuccessful–returned to Monterey empty handed. To his surprise, the business was closed, La Esperanza shuttered, and no partners accountable due to questionable deed and title shuffling by the partners. Time passed as the property moved through questionable sales and re-deeding which ultimately found Vincent Rodrigues living at 740 Ocean View Avenue.

In 1928 there still was no legal settlement of the claims of ownership of 740 when Vincent Rodriguez was about to sell it to Ed Ricketts for the new site of his Pacific Biological Laboratories. An inept and careless attorney for Joseph Rodrigues failed to stop the sale of the property. The Joseph Rodriguez family lost the case and the sale was made to Ricketts. The rest, as they say "...is history."

Magnificent, painstaking historical research by Ms. Robin Rodriguez Aeschliman, the granddaughter of Joseph Rodriguez, illuminates Ed Ricketts' acquisition of the "La Esperanza." She is proud of her family's ironic role in the survival of Ed Ricketts' Lab. We may never have known a Ricketts or Steinbeck otherwise.

[See Page 137; Bibliography Page 139]

In 1929, Carmel blacksmith, Francis Whitaker, forged the latches, hinges and fireplace hood for an "art studio" for his close friend Jack Calvin's wife, Sasha. Whitaker reported that it was here at a 1930 party of the Calvin's group of friends that John Steinbeck and Ed Ricketts were introduced. Calvin's group adopted Ed Ricketts' lab for parties after Jack and Sasha moved to Sitka, Alaska, in 1932.　　　*Tom & Margie Morjig photo [2003-054-001]*

Salinas-born Pacific Grove writer, John Steinbeck.　　　*[85-028-001]*

For many years there was a controversy over just how John Steinbeck met Ed Ricketts. John Steinbeck wrote that it happened in a dentist's office, but after all John does write fiction. The actual location and conditions under which Steinbeck met Ed Ricketts WERE only confirmed in 1991.

A "push down" cottage in Carmel Woods bought by San Francisco Bay Area businessman Tom Morjig and his wife, Margie, was restored instead of replaced with the ostentatious "lot-line to lot-line" vacation dachas that dominate so much of Carmel-By-The-Sea. Tom Morjig's thorough research on the cottage included available title research and permits over the years, but nothing existed about its original construction.

The historic and literary value of the cottage came to light when a former resident stopped at its Dutch door one day to say she had grown up in the cottage from the age of five. Dina Bohn Concoran was able to provide valuable new information that a Carmel blacksmith and political activist, Francis Whitacker, helped build it and forged the door hardware and fireplace hood. Morjig located the famous master blacksmith, Francis Whitaker, in Colorado, who personally reported to him that the "art studio" was built in 1929 for Jack Calvin's wife, Sasha, and that he was at the party at Calvin's studio in 1930 when Ricketts and Steinbeck—to become two of America's intellectual giants—were introduced.

When the Calvin's moved to Sitka, Alaska, in 1932, Ed Ricketts' lab on Cannery Row became the new gathering site for the intellectual and artistic group. Published in 1939, "Between Pacific Tides" was co-authored by Calvin. Two years later Ricketts would co-author "Sea of Cortez" with Steinbeck.

The Ricketts family C. 1932: Ed Jr., Anna, (front) Cornelia ("Rikki"), Nancy, and Ed at the Carmel home of Eds' brother-in-law, Fred Strong. [99-016-008]

Ed's mother, Alice B. Ricketts, with Ed and his son, Ed. Jr. in Carmel Woods with Ed's 1937 Ford V-8 coupe.   Fred Strong photo 1937[95-033-003]

Ed in Carmel Woods by brother-in-law Fred Strong.   [95-033-002]

Frankie Bergara, center, and fellow cannery friends—not in their work clothes—posing in front of the lot next to Ed Ricketts' Pacific Biological Laboratories. This little known lot remained vacant except for the cypress trees until 1946. Grace Bergara *photo, 1935.* [97-108-001]

The Cannery Row lab was originally a single-story house purchased by Pacific Biological Laboratories in 1928 in a relocation from Pacific Grove. The building was lifted and the laboratory portion constructed on the lower floor. Fred Strong *photo* [95-033-0011]

The Del Mar Canning Company caught fire on November 25, 1936. The fire next-door spread and completely destroyed the original, stucco Lab and one of the most extensive collections of marine invertebrate biology research in existence anywhere. Fortunately, his manuscript for his pioneering intertidal marine biological text book, "Between Pacific Tides," was at Stanford University Press. His extensive library was destroyed in the inferno. Morgan [93-044-001]

Del Vista Packing Company, a concrete reduction plant, was constructed next to the Lab in 1946. Ed's insurance was insufficient to rebuild the stucco Lab after the 1936 fire, and with the Depression still raging, he settled for its simpler wood-siding reconstruction.   *Ed Ricketts, Jr. photo [98-083-012]*

Ed Ricketts' living room with its fold-down "drop leaf" table and book shelves, in the rebuilt Lab.   *1947 Photo by Ed Ricketts Jr.* [81-021-071]

Ed's hemp-rope suspended mattress and its Hudson Bay blanket, beneath a small copy of Elwood Graham's portrait of John after the trip to the Sea of Cortez. Ed kept it to cajole John, who was uneasy with the image. The simple furnishings of a Renaissance man.   *Ed Ricketts, Jr.* [81-021-074]

Edward F. Ricketts, circa 1936. The real life scientist and ecologist would become six major characters in Steinbeck fiction in what could be highest synthesis of science and literature in the American experience.   *Fred Strong photo [95-033-01]*

Flora Woods, Cannery Row's magnanimous madam in a 1944 photo, after her days in "the business" were over and four years before her death in near poverty.   *[85-024-001]*

Ed's Lab and its shed with the Lone Star (Bear Flag) of Flora Wood (Dora Flood) across the street; the "vacant lot" and Black Cypress, and up the embankment above the tracks, the Palace Flophouse next to the Joss House from China Point in its third and last location.   *Ted McKay [84-096-001]*

Steinbeck "Cannery Row" sites in this photo:
(Numbers are keyed to the Map Index on Page 120)

Please note these locator numbers have changed from
previous editions due to the addition of sites included.

12. The Palace Flophouse
21. Dora Flood's Bear Flag Restaurant (Lone Star Cafe)
18. The Black Cypress
18. The "vacant" lot
10. The fish meal barn described as the Palace Flophouse
20. Doc's Western Biological Laboratory
15. Wing Chong Market
14. La Ida Cafe
 7. Hediondo Cannery

Ted McKay [83-006-062]

Some of Ed Ricketts' laboratory glass and equipment used for preserving, identifying and preparing his specimens for sale.   Fred Strong   [95-033-005]

Ed's close friend, Richie Lovejoy, drew many of the scientific illustrations in Ed's "Between Pacific Tides," in the Lab with Ed and a ray.   [81-021-070]

The Del Monte Forest sloping to Carmel Beach, the treeless Carmel Point, and the Carmel River flowing past the Martin Ranch–now Mission Ranch– to the sea at Carmel River Beach.
1924 Russell Aero Photo. [81-006-026]

Another not-so-fictional locale from Steinbeck's "Cannery Row" is the area of the frog hunt in Carmel Valley. The lower Hatton Ranch is seen at the entrance to the valley on Carmel Valley Road at Highway One in 1945.
George Seideneck [72-003-062]

The Wing Chong Market of the Yee Family could not have been described more accurately than by John Steinbeck.   George Robinson photo [81-021-088]

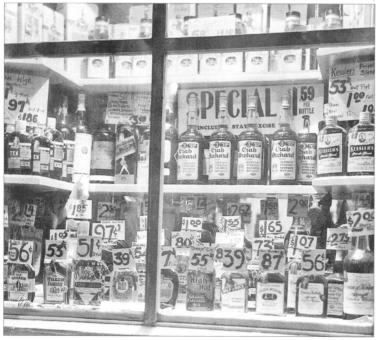

The elixirs of cannery life, like the "Old Tennis Shoes" whisky of Steinbeck's only slightly fictional "Cannery Row"—aged a whole three weeks! Alcohol was often the anesthesia of choice for some men working 12-16 hours a day at the gritty, hard labor of depression era cannery life. It's toll was high on families and funds: almost all of the bottles in this view of the Wing Chong Market window cost more than an hour's gritty, hard labor wages in one of the Row's canneries.   [2001-020-121]

Cannery workers at the A. F. of L. Fish Cannery Workers Union office at the Ocean View Hotel.   [85-029-001]

THERE IS NO "DOC RICKETTS"

The major defining point in John Steinbeck's "Cannery Row" is the focal character of "Doc." Around him, the rest of one of the greatest stories in American fiction is constructed and unfolds. John Steinbeck's official biographer, Professor Jackson Benson, assessed John's greatest works in this order: "Of Mice and Men"..."Grapes of Wrath"...and "Cannery Row."

Until that moment at the annual Steinbeck Festival in Salinas (at the release of his Steinbeck Biography in 1984) when he replied to a question from the audience as to what he, personally—as Steinbeck's official biographer—considered his most important works, little had been considered of the import of a relatively obscure and seemingly lighthearted and nostalgic flashback on America at a simpler time. Its inclusion in Steinbeck's top three by Jack Benson shed new light and interest on a far more complex and sophisticated literary work than had been appreciated—at least until then.

John writes his editor, Pat Covici, at Viking Press that he has written it on four levels. Susan Shillinglaw of the Steinbeck Studies Center at San Jose State University has furthered that case with an introduction to the Penguin 1994 edition of "Cannery Row" in paperback—featuring a Life Magazine feature photo by Peter Stackpole on the cover, of no less than Harold Otis "Gabe" Bicknell: John' self professed model for Mack in "Cannery Row."

Nowhere in "Cannery Row" is there a Doc Ricketts. Only a Doc. Ed was known to by his friends as, simply, Ed. It is surely because the character of "Doc" was constructed so obviously on Ed Ricketts—even to the use of his real name in its dedication: "For Ed Ricketts, who knows why or should"—that over time the two would blur. But this mingling of the real and fictional roles of Ed Ricketts does create a significant point requiring comment and clarification.

Ed Ricketts was an accomplished marine biologist, without a degree after two years at the University of Chicago, but none the less an acute and systematic observer of the intertidal zones from which he collected his livelihood and his scientific status. He came to Pacific Grove in 1923 with a partner, Albert E. Galigher, to set up a biological supply business providing specimens to science classes, schools and laboratories all over the country. Without academic credentials, however, he was initially considered by the tenured academic scientists at Hopkins Marine Station of Stanford University, as only slightly less than a poacher of the intertidal.

The decade of the 1930s, in the middle of the Great Depression, Ed Ricketts amassed the most complete intertidal record of the West Coast of North America in existence anywhere—at any university. In this turbulent decade Ed Ricketts succeeded in turning the science of marine biology on hits head. All consolidated in a fitful biological supply business run from a small stucco home and laboratory squeezed between sardine factories in a canyon of canneries that lined Ocean View Avenue in Monterey.

Beyond his scientific interests, however, Ed displayed what Katharine Rodger calls, "The Renaissance Man of Cannery Row" in her work of his collected letters. His interest in art, philosophy, classical music, poetry—particularly the Chinese of Li Po and the Tao—and his sincere touch with people of virtually all ages, made Ed the center of a certain universe on Cannery Row and around Monterey. This was the man John Steinbeck was introduced to at a party at Jack Calvin's cottage in Carmel in 1930. Neither would be the same again.

Ed Ricketts in the Lab, circa 1936, by Bryant Fitch.   [81-021-078]

The symbiotic relationship between writer and scientist is not as simple a dichotomy as might be thought. John Steinbeck had shown a facility and interest in science and biology well before his both intermittent and turbulent Stanford years. He professed that had writing not worked out for him, he may have joined his friend and mentor, Ed Ricketts, in the biological supply business. John was, in fact, a very capable amateur biologist by any measure—one talented enough to contribute effectively to the Sea of Cortez mission.

Ed, on the other hand, admired John enormously for his skill and command of the crafted word. Ed's scientific and philosophic composition suffered from a stilted and tortured expression too frequent among scientists. Yet his concepts were revolutionary and he was committed to their expression.

Ed's manual of the West Coast intertidal zone was published in 1939 by Stanford University Press, with much help from John Steinbeck, pushing Stanford to do it. It is a tribute to Ed that generations of senior marine biologists gladly admit that it was Ed Ricketts and his landmark work, "Between Pacific Tides," that inspired them into the field. The manuscript for Ed's life work was at Stanford Press when the catastrophic fire in 1936 took his lab and all its contents—including the most complete marine biological record of West Coast intertidal invertebrate life in existence at the time.

Those that knew him called him Ed. Readers of Steinbeck's fiction call him "Doc." Overwhelming numbers of people who came to know Ed as "Doc" are principally responsible for creating the misnomer "Doc" Ricketts–which appears nowhere in Steinbeck's fiction. The result is an unfortunate confusion that true Ricketts fans are dedicated to correct.

Since the Cannery Row Foundation was established in 1983 it has endeavored to correct the popular misnomer of Steinbeck's fictional Doc from Ed Ricketts the great pioneer ecological scientist. There is no Doc Ricketts.

SEA OF CORTEZ

The publication of John Steinbeck's "Grapes of Wrath" in 1939 was met by anger and virulent protests in California's agricultural circles. In reaction to Steinbeck's literary exposé´ of the desperation and abuse of the ragged westward migration of pitifully disenfranchised farmers from America's Dust Bowl, angry mobs publicly burned his books in his home town of Salinas and in other enraged California farm communities.

To many of those whom he exposed, Steinbeck was rebuked as a Communist and traitor to his agricultural heritage. John faced death threats and at one point applied for and was issued a permit to carry a concealed weapon, an aging hand gun of dubious integrity. The growing popularity of his cause and its reaction was heightened by the release of "Grapes of Wrath" by 20th Century Fox starring Henry Fonda. John was no longer safe anywhere near Salinas which precipitated a plan of escape from the troubling and fearful heat of public controversy: a marine biological expedition to Mexico like several John and Ed made in the 1930s. Ed's time on the "Grampus" may account for the decision to conduct this study aboard a boat from the Monterey sardine fleet.

The opportunity to conduct a detailed exploration of the Gulf of California's shores by boat rather than the very limited road access to otherwise remote prime collection spots–and of special importance–to remove John from the pressure and threats of his literary and political maelstrom proved impossible to resist. Plans were coming together quickly until an unexpected difficulty in chartering one of Monterey's nearly 80 vessels arose.

Steinbeck knew many of the Monterey fleet skippers from hanging around the waterfront and the same bars they did, and getting to know some well enough to have a glass of red with them on their seiners. It came as a surprise that none of them would take the off-season charter to the Sea of Cortez. In the wake of "Grapes of Wrath" and Steinbeck's labor-friendly record, Monterey's very conservative Sicilian boat owners considered Steinbeck a Communist and as a group they refused to accept his charter requests. One last Sicilian skipper was reluctantly considering the charter, but suddenly doubled his price: caving in to the unanimous Sicilian boat owner' pressures–and saving face by changing his mind about the cost to Steinbeck. So, there were no other boats available to charter to the Sea of Cortez; or so it seemed.

Toby Street, Steinbeck's close friend and lawyer at Hudson Martin & Ferrante was helped by partner Peter Ferrante who contacted his uncle, Orazio Enea, President of the Monterey Boat Owners Association. Enea recommended they see Tony Berry. Though a Croatian, Berry had the good fortune to be in the Sicilian dominated fleet by virtue of his 1936 marriage to Orazio Enea's daughter, Rose. An orderly, straightforward deal was drawn up with Tony Berry and Steinbeck, each agreeing to the terms of responsibilities of both parties. The deal was promptly signed and activities began at once to buy supplies and prepare the Western Flyer for her six week charter to the Sea of Cortez, the historic traditional Mexican name for today's Gulf of California. Carol Steinbeck insisted on being along though women on boats violated many a seaman's worst fears. But come she did, some saying with the misguided belief that six weeks on a boat loaded with beer with six men and hard work to do every day in the tidelands of Baja might save a failing marriage. It did not, with plenty of difficulties during the entire trip. But the Western Flyer would soon become world-famous because of the troubled charter.

Adapted from Google Earth

Deck hands Ratzi "Tiny" Colletto and Horace "Sparky" Enea.
[Reprinted by permission of the Martha Heasley Cox Center for Steinbeck Studies, San Jose State University]

In the spring of 1940, two published authors took a voyage of travel and research to Baja California's Sea of Cortez. One had just published "Grapes of Wrath," the other "Between Pacific Tides." Both had looked forward to this trip since the mid 1930's—part of Ed Ricketts' plan to chart the entire West Coast for publication of a series of manuals on the Pacific inter-tidal zones from Baja California to the Queen Charlotte Islands of British Columbia and beyond to Sitka and the Bering Sea.

The trip was financed by John Steinbeck, organized by Ed Ricketts and conducted on board a Monterey purse seiner skippered by the afore mentioned Croatian, Tony Berry from Tacoma, Washington. It was a nearly new boat, 76 feet long, 25 feet in the beam, powered by a 165 horsepower Atlas diesel. On board were John, his wife Carol, Ed Ricketts, skipper Tony Berry, mechanic Hal "Tex" Travis, and deckhands Horace "Sparky" Enea and "Tiny" Colletto.

The record of this colorful adventure is recounted in the two-part book "Sea of Cortez" resulting from this expedition and Steinbeck's only co-authored work. Slightly less than half is the narrative of the trip. The slightly larger back-half is a rich and extensively illustrated catalogue of an extraordinary number of new species observed and collected. Subject matter of the narrative was not, however, confined to the scientific. The narrative also deals with description of the remoteness of the gulf, with the relationship of themselves and the Western Flyer as part of it by being in it, with survival of species sharing it while reflecting the similarly interconnected nature of humanity chafing at sharing the globe. It reflects solemnly on approach of war, of human conduct—and a soaring introduction to holistic thinking as an anthem to a new, ecological philosophy. It also includes the raucous, sometimes bawdy, and frequently hilarious episodes of the Western Flyer's wiley and notorious deckhands.

"Sea of Cortez" was published in early December, 1941, almost as bombs were falling on Pearl Harbor—relegating it to all but complete obscurity for long after the duration of the war. However, some of it's first printing of 1000 copies reached into the biological community as well as avid Steinbeck devotees. It's wider recognition would only come after Ed Ricketts' death in 1948, as Steinbeck struggled with the loss of his mentor and muse and Viking Press pressured him to get back into the very competitive writing scene. That was most easily accomplished by going back to the well of previous material: "Sea of Cortez."

In 1951, Steinbeck succeeding in getting Ed Ricketts Jr. to sign-off on removing his father's scientific back-half of the book. Viking Press then published just the voyage's narrative as "The Log From the sea of Cortez"—with only Steinbeck's authorship. It began the book's broad favor with Steinbeck's readership, but was haunted by the knowledge of some in the Ricketts-Steinbeck world that the narrative contained a great deal of Ricketts' previously published or circulated thought, philosophy, and ecological vision.

There is absolutely no doubt, however, the log was a thoughtful and genuine collaboration by both men. The philosophical and mystical side of Ed Ricketts appears through the material in forms like "non-teleological thinking," attributed by some unknowing critics at the time as the work and thought of Steinbeck, the book's writer.

The voyage was a notable scientific success of major proportions but John and Carol fared so badly as their troubled marriage continued breaking apart that Carol is unmentioned by Steinbeck in the account of the trip in "The Sea of Cortez." John wrote the book from Ed Ricketts' notes and Tony Berry's skipper's log at the cottage of Ellwood and Barbara Graham (Judith Deim) on Lobos Street in the hilly pine woods above Cannery Row. John sat for a portrait by Ellwood but disliked it and required him to do another while he sat at his writing. Judith Deim also painted John's portrait as he was writing; her's survives at the Center for Steinbeck Studies at San Jose State University, California.

John and Carol Steinbeck on the flying bridge of Skipper Tony Berry's "Western Flyer" in Monterey harbor on its return from the March-April 1940 voyage to the Sea of Cortez. After the voyage John and Carol's troubled marriage would soon unravel completely.   Fred Strong photo [95-033-008]

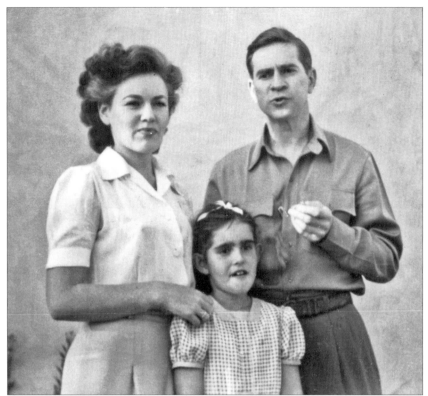

Toni Jackson and her daughter, Kay, with Ed.   *Fred Strong photo [99-026-029]*

Corporal Ed Ricketts, 1943, with Tony's daughter, Kay.
Fred Strong photo [99-026-003]

In early in 1940, Virginia Scardighli, one of Ed's circle and wife of Remo Scardighli–designer of the new Lab for Ed after the 1936 fire–introduced Ed to her best friend, divorcée Toni Jackson from San Francisco. Smart and attractive, Toni quickly became Ed's unwed companion from 1940 until 1947. She was attractive and smart, in her youth scoring so high on intelligence tests that she became a participant in Stanford's prestigious Lewis Termin Genetic Studies of Genius. It ran in the family as it was her naturalist father, Theodore Solomans, who conceived the idea and explored routes of what would become the John Muir Trail though California's High Sierras.

The publication of John Steinbeck's "Grapes of Wrath" in 1939 was met with angry protests in California's agricultural circles. In reaction to Steinbeck's literary expose of desperation and abuse of the ragged westward migration of disenfranchised farmers from America's Dust Bowl, his books were publicly burned in his home town of Salinas, as well as across enraged California farm communities.

To many of those whom he exposed, Steinbeck was rebuked as a Communist and traitor to his agricultural heritage. John faced death threats and at one point applied for and was issued a permit to carry a concealed weapon, an aging handgun of dubious integrity. The growing popularity of his cause, and its reaction, was heightened by the release of "Grapes of Wrath" by 20th Century Fox starring Henry Fonda. John was no longer safe anywhere near Salinas which precipitated a plan of escape from the troubling and fearful heat of public controversy: a marine biological expedition to Mexico like several John and Ed made in the 1930s. But this time not by automobile but by boat, as addressed in the previous chapter.

The deeply troubled Steinbeck marriage did not survive for long after the voyage to the Gulf of California. Her presence on the voyage is not mentioned anywhere in John's narrative of the trip and her further work for John was no longer possible due to his living with, and planning his marriage to, the much younger Gwyn Conger with whom Steinbeck was overwhelmingly smitten.

Toni felt in her element when it fell to her to take on the editing and typing of the manuscript of the "Sea of Cortez," work which would always have been done by Carol Steinbeck. Toni typed the complete manuscript for "Sea of Cortez" from Steinbeck's cramped and miniscule handwriting that John had composed from Ed's field notes and skipper Tony Berry's captain's log. John had kept none on the trip. Ricketts was 45 when he was drafted into the U.S. Army a second time. He had been conscripted late in WWI, never leaving the U.S. This time Ed spent 1942-1943 at the Presidio of Monterey induction center processing medical tests on recruits on the way to basic training. He refused to use the Army's "sink test"—meaning if the recruit's urine sample went down the sink, they were in the Army. He was diligent and dedicated in his lab tests, sometimes thousands of war-bound thousand recruits a day. He even identified a case of leprosy at first disbelieved by his superiors. The Army did permit Ed to live at home on Cannery Row at Pacific Biological Laboratories.

After Ed's discharge from the U.S. Army in late 1943 his Pacific Biological Laboratories business was unable to survive without Ed taking part-time work at Cal-Pac's Plant #106 chemical lab performing complex chemical tests on batches of fish-meal for content and potency. Outgoing chemist Norman Buell was a phenom at the process which required complex and rapid results which Norman patiently taught Ed how to perform and calculate quickly. That was about all that was going well.

Toni wrote fairly frequently for the Monterey Herald and Monterey Peninsula magazine "What's Doing?" to help out in these difficult times. Early in her relationship with Ed it was discovered that Toni's daughter, Kay, had an inoperable brain tumor which added more strain to their relationship in a worsening situation at Pacific Biological Laboratories.

Cal-Pac Plant 106 chemistry lab. San Xavier warehouse in the background. Mortimer P. Starr [2019-40-0002]

Norman Buell and Ed at Cal-Pac Plant #106 chem lab. Mortimer P. Starr [2019-40-0001]

Ed and Toni separated in 1947 after Toni's daughter, Kay, died of a brain tumor. Toni worked for John Steinbeck for a while in New York but returned to Monterey only to find Ed married a young woman half his age, 25 tear-old student at University of California, Alice Campbell. She was accompanying Ed on a trip in January 1948, when they were married in an impromptu ceremony while passing through Barstow, California. Unaware that he had failed to complete his divorce papers from his previous marriage—to Anna Macker, the mother of his children—his error went undetected at the time and didn't become a major complication until Ed's death after his collision with the Del Monte Express on May 8, 1948. His new "wife" was, of course, young, grief-stricken, embarrassed, and legally deprived of what little of value Ed left behind—which only added to the incredulity, shock and sadness of what had so suddenly come to pass. Ed was gone and a mess left behind.

Ed and Toni at the Starr home before Christmas 1944. Mortimer P. Starr [2019-40-003]

Alice Campbell Ricketts in 1947, never expecting Ed's death on May 11th, 1948. [81-021-0076]

Alice Ricketts. Ed Ricketts Jr. [97-023-0001]

On the evening of May 8th, 1948, Ed Ricketts started his old Buick and drove from the Lab toward town on Ocean View Avenue. Beyond the San Xavier cannery and the Tevis estate houses it turns to climb the hill, to the intersection with Drake and Wave Avenues. Just uphill from the intersection was an unmarked but familiar rail crossing. It was at this fateful spot Ed's car was struck by the evening Del Monte Express train inbound to Pacific Grove. The Oxnard cannery warehouse obscured the track view toward town and the train struck Ed's car before he was able to exit it. It is probable that his car had stalled and Ed tried too long to restart it before trying to get out through the driver's-side door.

The impact of the steam engine crushed Ed between the driver's door and the door post as it pushed the car several hundred feet down the track before coming to an emergency stop. A crowd of stunned residents and some cannery workers gathered. Police photos show the rider's side door open and Ed lying crumpled in the grass with serious head and internal injuries. Some believe had Ed stayed in the car, or tried to exit the old car on the rider's side, he would likely have survived.

Ed died of his injuries on May 11th, in spite of valiant efforts to save him. John Steinbeck flew immediately from New York, but did not arrive before Ed passed away, days before his birthday on May 14th. John, as the major financial partner in Pacific Bio-

logical Laboratories, went through Ed's combination office, lab and home at 800 Ocean View Avenue, sorting, and purging Ed's records, correspondence, research, and scientific materials. He was assisted by a friend and co-worker of Ed's at Cal-Pac, George Robinson. Together they disposed of materials Steinbeck excluded from distribution to friends and family and materials for Hopkins Marine Station.

The Lab sat vacant several years after Ed's death, until rented by a Monterey High School teacher, Harlan Watkins. He succeeded in buying it in 1956 from Yock "Jack" Yee, the son of Won Yee, the Lee Chong in Steinbeck's "Cannery Row." A group of Watkins' friends met at the Lab on Wednesday evenings, played jazz records and explored all manner of conversation before adjourning to Neil DeVaughn's restaurant in the Ocean View Hotel for mock turtle soup and fondue.

When Harlan announced he was getting married his fiancé Louise refused to inhabit the Lab. For the group it appeared to be a lose-lose: if she moved in they could no longer use the Lab; if she did not it would have to be sold. They were about to lose their clubhouse when group member Ed Haber (in early development of Quail Lodge in Carmel Valley) figured out how they could pool resources to obtain a loan to buy the Lab from Harlan to keep their private men's club. Few know that enabled the Lab group to become the source of the Monterey Jazz Festival.

This view of the back of the Lab looks down on the shed roof behind the Lab covering concrete specimen tanks Ed Ricketts used to sort and segregate specimens collected on his local and distant excursions. The tanks were an important reason Ed bought the property.
Harlan Watkins photo [98-007-001]

The canyon-like view from the Lab between the Del Vista and Del Mar canneries photographed by Monterey High School teacher, Harlan Watkins, who rented the vacant lab after Ed Ricketts' death.
Harlan Watkins [98-007-002]

This view down the unfinished Irving Avenue from Wave Street shows the boarded up Pacific Biological Laboratories, the concrete warehouse replacement for the Lone Star Cafe of Flora Woods, and a corner of the actual "Palace Flophouse"—the name and location, but not the fish meal-storage building Steinbeck described in "Cannery Row" which is off this photo to the left on Wave Street, looking down across the tracks at the back of Wing Chong Market.
George Robinson [81-021-0109]

Monterey officer Frank Marinello with the injured Ed Ricketts at the site of the collision with the Del Monte Express, May 8th, 1948. Ed's old Buick stalled on the grade crossing at Drake Avenue and Wave Street. If he had not tried so long to restart it, or had stayed in the car, it is likely he would have survived. He was crushed between the driver's door and the door post by the engine, sustaining injuries from which he died two days later   Wm. L. Morgan [2008-007-001]

The publication of Steinbeck's "Cannery Row" in 1945 coincided with the zenith of Monterey's sardine fishing and canning era as wartime production enabled its proclamation as "Sardine Capital of the World." The echoes of this proud boast had hardly faded when the Monterey sardine industry, and the community it supported, were visited by an irony and agony of catastrophic proportions.

The 1945-46 season was nearly half of the volume of the previous year's catch. A stunned industry held its breath and awaited the 1946-47 season: it was to be the worst since 1922! And the 1947-48 season was to be, unbelievably, even worse yet! "Table 8" provides an all-too-vivid picture of the rise and fall of an industry predicated upon the impossible.

POST MORTEM

The honest fear that the worst had really happened was settling in on Monterey. No longer an academic argument between businessmen and biologists, the sardine simply wasn't there for the capture. Ed Ricketts' death was somehow almost symbolic of the unexpected, impossible tragedy for which the cannery barons and fishing families of Monterey were totally unprepared.

Angelo Lucido, Sal Ventimiglia, Knut Hovden, and the remaining canners desperately attempted trucking iced fish from the Santa Barbara area, and as far south as Port Hueneme. Spoilage, transport costs and insufficient volume doomed such attempts by an industry that had already had its chance to anticipate such contingencies, but had not.

As canneries closed, most of them into bankruptcy, a ghost town pallor and despair hung heavily over Ocean View Avenue as strong as the former smell of baking sardine meal. It was going and would soon be gone, this street of the sardine.

The Lone Star Cafe of madam Flora Woods became a concrete fish meal warehouse. The La Ida Cafe, closed by the War, had a sign reading "Rooms For Rent." The Wing Chong Market was soon to be liquidated by Won Yee's son, Jack.

The 1951 filming of the RKO movie "Clash By Night," a production by the first female producer in Hollywood, Louella Parsons' daughter Harriet, could scarcely find enough fish for the documentary-like opening fishing and canning scenes of a hardy coastal community. This classic film starred Barbara Stanwyck, Robert Ryan, Paul Douglas, and introduced Marilyn Monroe, in her co-starring debut—as a cannery worker on the cutting machines...in an industry still unwilling to accept it was in its last futile gasps.

Southern California waters sustained a reducing level of sardine landings into the mid-1950s but then it quickly followed the same fate as Monterey into utter disbelief that the "Silver Tide" had actually ceased.

While sardine supplies were holding out further south, desperate canners began trucking fish from southern ports, such as Port Hueneme, to Monterey for processing. Spoilage, low volume, and high transportation costs doomed the efforts.
[74-012-013]

HISTORICAL REVIEW 1916–1968

TABLE 8
SEASONAL LANDINGS IN TONS
Sardines

Season*	Reduction ships	San Francisco area	Monterey area	Los Angeles area	San Diego area	Total tons
1916–17	----	----	7,710	17,380	2,440	27,530
1917–18	----	70	23,810	41,340	7,360	72,580
1918–19	----	450	35,750	32,530	6,810	75,540
1919–20	----	1,000	43,040	16,580	6,410	67,030
1920–21	----	230	24,960	11,740	1,520	38,450
1921–22	----	80	16,290	19,220	910	36,500
1922–23	----	110	29,210	33,170	2,620	65,110
1923–24	----	190	45,920	35,040	2,780	83,930
1924–25	----	560	67,310	96,330	8,820	173,020
1925–26	----	560	69,010	61,990	5,710	137,270
1926–27	----	3,520	81,860	64,720	2,110	152,210
1927–28	----	16,690	98,020	67,900	4,650	187,260
1928–29	----	13,520	120,290	119,250	1,420	254,480
1929–30	----	21,960	160,050	140,540	2,620	325,170
1930–31	10,960	25,970	109,620	38,490	80	185,120
1931–32	31,040	21,607	69,078	42,656	264	164,645
1932–33	58,790	18,634	89,599	83,605	62	250,690
1933–34	67,820	36,336	152,480	125,047	1,746	383,429
1934–35	112,040	68,477	230,854	178,818	4,865	595,054
1935–36	150,830	76,147	184,470	138,400	10,651	560,498
1936–37	235,610	141,099	206,706	138,115	4,594	726,124
1937–38	67,580	133,718	104,936	109,947	383	416,564
1938–39	43,890	201,200	180,994	146,403	2,800	575,287
1939–40	----	212,453	227,874	96,827	112	537,266
1940–41	----	118,092	165,698	175,592	1,202	460,584
1941–42	----	186,589	250,287	148,912	1,585	587,373
1942–43	----	115,884	184,399	201,510	2,868	504,661
1943–44	----	126,512	213,616	135,311	2,690	478,129
1944–45	----	136,598	237,246	178,294	2,767	554,905
1945–46	----	84,103	145,519	173,110	951	403,683
1946–47	----	2,869	31,391	194,774	4,768	233,802
1947–48	----	94	17,630	101,154	2,463	121,341
1948–49	----	112	47,862	131,830	3,922	183,726
1949–50	----	17,442	131,769	186,433	3,281	338,925
1950–51	----	12,727	33,699	303,752	2,910	353,088
1951–52	----	82	15,897	111,774	1,351	129,104
1952–53	----	----	49	5,635	27	5,711
1953–54	----	----	58	4,111	323	4,492
1954–55	----	----	856	67,099	510	68,465
1955–56	----	----	518	73,943	----	74,461
1956–57	----	----	63	33,564	16	33,643
1957–58	----	----	17	22,255	----	22,272
1958–59	----	----	24,701	79,264	6	103,971
1959–60	----	----	16,109	21,146	1	37,256
1960–61	----	----	2,340	26,436	102	28,878
1961–62	----	----	2,231	23,295	2	25,528
1962–63	----	----	1,211	2,961	----	4,172
1963–64	----	----	1,015	1,895	32	2,942
1964–65	----	----	308	5,717	78	6,103
1965–66	----	----	151	535	33	719
1966–67	----	----	23	311	10	344
1967–68	----	----	10	61	----	71

* Season June through the following May.

Department of Fish and Game, Fish Bulletin No. 149: The California Marine Fish Catch for 1968 and Historical Review 1916-1968, by Richard F. G. Heimann and John G. Carlisle, Jr., 1970. A statistical study of disaster.

TRUCKIN'

Little can be said that this photo of one of the Hovden trucks being unloaded on Ocean View Avenue doesn't implicitly say: less than a lampara lighter of sardines, hundreds of miles by road from fresh capture further south, sluiced into a proud cannery accustomed to dozens of boatloads loads larger than this per day. The obviously futile effort to keep Monterey canning by this method of delivery to the sardine factories of Cannery Row was a cruel and ignominious punishment for the industry's ignorance, greed and arrogance.

Of all the photographs in this book this one is among the most poignant because it illustrates the futility of not having managed a potentially unlimited resource intelligently upon which the entire industry and dependents predicated their prosperity and survival. Now even the desperate trucking of sardines from Southern California was doomed to failure and yet, unbelievably, Monterey was still totally unprepared with an alternative to this disaster for which it had decades to devise contingencies.

Just as the reality of the fishery collapse began to set in, RKO, the Hollywood studio owned by Howard Hughes, decided to make a film about a seaside fishing and canning community. With the film, "Clash By Night," Harriet Parsons, the daughter of Hearst Hollywood columnist, Louella Parsons, became the first female producer in Hollywood. This last opportunity for Monterey's fishing and canning industry to play a role as its old self was fortuitous. Its opening documentary scenes are a memory of Cannery Row's river of silver fish from catch to can. There were barely enough sardines caught to make the film possible. Then they were gone and no number of trucks from the south could replace the purse seiners at the hoppers off Cannery Row.

Cal-Pac waits silently to resume canning and shipping the silver tide that now arrived by truck.
Robert Lewis/THC photo [2009-003-053]

Absolute disaster had become absolute reality as the true cost of continued operation of canneries suddenly located hundreds of miles from its source of fish became apparent. Trucking fish proved unworkable due to low volume, high spoilage, and steep transportation costs.
Fred Harbick photo [73-006-049]

The RKO crew and a crowd of Monterey spectators watch the night-time filming of the closing scenes of "Clash By Night" at Wharf #2. Barbara Stanwyck and Robert Ryan are on the purse seiner; Harriet Parsons, Hollywood's first female producer, is the lone woman among the men on the left of this photo. One of Hollywood's most famous—and difficult—directors, Fritz Lang, is in the checked wool shirt at center.   Donn Clickard [81-041-027]

Harriet Parsons, daughter of Hearst Newspaper columnist Louella Parsons, produced a film in Monterey in mid-October, 1951, for RKO Pictures. Harriet was the first female producer in Hollywood and worked for mogul Howard Hughes. The film, "Clash By Night, " starred Barbara Stanwyck, Robert Ryan, Paul Douglas, Keith Andes, and—in her first dramatic co-starring role—Marilyn Monroe.

The opening scenes of the film is a documentary style sequence of a fishing port with a fleet of boats going out to sea under dark skies, the setting of nets and hauling of silver fish into holds, and the unloading of fish at the canneries of an anonymous fishing town. This documentary-style opening of the film followed the path of the silver fish into the cannery, to the cutting lines, where rows of women at cutting machines placed the fish in "slots" (see page 74) for cutting prior to packing. One of them is Marilyn Monroe in her first co-starring role, on the slots at the San Xavier cannery. Hollywood contributed a valuable look at the fishing and canning process in setting the opening scenes of this motion picture. Filming the fishing and canning sequences, however, was anything but easy in the 1951 season.

An industry accustomed to 200,000 tons of fish per season was experiencing a season destined to end with less

than 16,000 tons. In her unpublished autobiography, Harriet Parsons bemoans the problems of having a fleet and a railroad at her disposal, but no fish for the scenes in the script. It was with great effort, and not a little cunning, that so few fish she and director Fritz Lang did finally obtain from the stricken fleet were made to look so plentiful as to belie the real scarcity of fish from in silver tide for which Monterey had become so internationally famous.

Some of the filming, however, became entertaining in its own right, when an enterprising canny worker, Jesse ("Tuto") Paredes, intentionally sent a can down the can chute sideways at the San Xavier cannery packing line, causing the line to be shut down—so all the cannery workers could rush to the windows to see Marilyn Monroe being filmed in a scene being shot on the street outside.

The legacy of RKO's 1952 black and white film "Clash By Night" is a celluloid record of the real-life skippers, fishermen, cannery workers and residents of Monterey's dying fishing and canning industry. Its scenes of Fisherman's Wharf and Cannery Row remain today as a lasting and accessible glimpse at Monterey as a working fishing port with its world-famous street at the heart of a tough industrial district that would all too soon simply die on its waterfront.

Ocean View Avenue from Hovden's looked like this at the end of each season. The last season would come far too soon.   Fred W. Harbick [73-130-005]

Words fail the obvious: the view from Prescott Avenue to Hovden's at the far end of the Row.   *George Robinson photo* [79-109-001]

FIREY OBITS

The plague of fire was to visit Cannery Row, claiming huge portions of this once indomitable street. Canneries and warehouses, reduction plants and sardine oil storage — an industry soaked in the oily breath of a zillion sardines and caked with the talcum-fine incendiary dust of its fish-meal dependent indulgence — fell easy prey to both arsonist and accident. The West Gate-Sun Harbor fire at the former Del Mar Cannery in December 1951 began the fire drill on Ocean View Avenue that would last well into the sixties.

As fate would have it, the once stately Ocean View Hotel of Mr. and Mrs. Wu—a symbol of Cannery Row's Chinese origins—was to bear silent witness to the funeral pyre of Monterey's once mighty sardine industry, and the dark and unspoken obituary to its blind and suicidal momentum and arrogance.

Its obituary may well have read: Farewell to the Old Row, buried by ledgers. Its legacy lies in the mosaic of the memories borne by its Alumni.

The West Gate-Sun Harbor fire at the former Del Mar Cannery was reported to be the largest food industry fire in the country's history at the time, with an estimated loss set at one and a half million dollars. There were inconclusive allegations of arson.
William L. Morgan [78-034-007]

The West Gate-Sun Harbor fire started the fire drill on Cannery Row that would last into its rebirth. The Del Monte Express train was held in Monterey because of the imminent danger of the cross-over collapse about to happen in this William L. Morgan photo.
[78-034-009]

Booth's reduction plant, even as the Edgewater Packing Company, succumbed to the inevitable.   *Robert Lewis/THC [2009-003-072]*

The venerable Monterey Canning Company waits like a sentinel for the return of the Silver Tide that does not come.   *Robert Lewis/THC [2009-003-001]*

Time standing still on old Ocean View Avenue.
Lewis/THC [2009-003-542]

Aeneas Sardine Products view to the Enterprise Packers and Peninsula Packing.
Howard Van Deren [93-032-001]

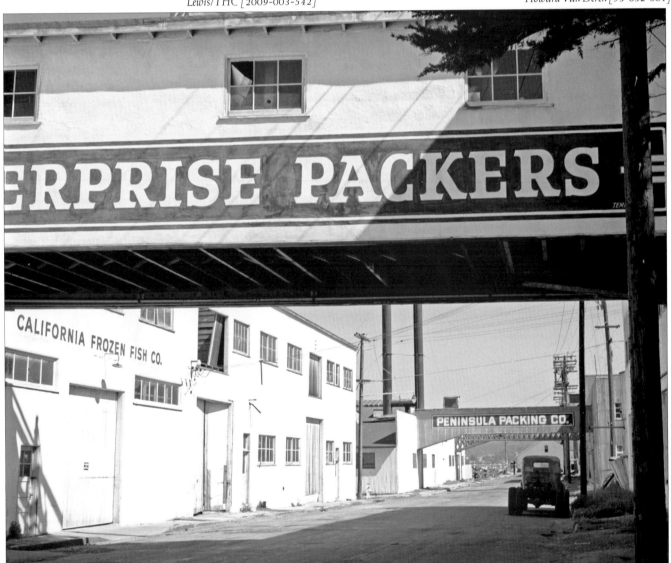

Not the street it used to be, nor was it the usual quiet between seasons: the unthinkable was upon it. This view looks toward the last blocks at the harbor end of the Row. Beyond Peninsula Packing, formerly E. B Gross, is the burned-out San Carlos cannery.
Robert Lewis/THC [2009-003-036]

George Leutzinger. Robert Lewis/THC [2009-003-326]

Equipment broker, Wesley Dodge, formed the Cannery Row Properties Company with George Leutzinger (above), buying all the closed and defunct canneries they could, then selling the idle canning and reduction equipment to Asian and South American operations for more than they paid for the property. They acquired over half the commercial property on the Old Row before its bulk sale to Ben Swig, the owner of San Francisco's Fairmont Hotel.

Wesley Dodge, whose Cannery Row Properties Company turned useless, dead canneries into vast commercial real estate holdings on the Row. Robert Lewis/THC [2009-003-327]

A salvaged reduction kiln waiting for shipment. Robert Lewis/THC [2009-003-108]

One of the CRP crews cutting up the canning lines for sale to overseas canners. Robert Lewis/THC [2000-003-153]

High style on the wrong side of the tracks. Diners enter pioneer restaurateur Neil DeVaughn's in the old Ocean View Hotel, 1958. Robert Lewis [2009-003-001]

In 1957, Kalisa Moore (1926-2009) leased a building for a new restaurant that opened July 5, 1958 on a street renamed Cannery Row. Her devotion to the street, its history, John Steinbeck and Ed Ricketts, earned her the acclaimed title "The Queen of Cannery Row." Robert Lewis/THC [2009-003-073]

As the "silver tide" subsided and then ceased, the lingering agony of the failed fishing and canning industry witnessed the amazing: an adventurous handful of business people, led by restaurateurs Neil DeVaughn and Kalisa Moore, pioneered the first restaurants on the Row at the turning point of the street. Ocean View Avenue became Cannery Row in January, 1958. The Old Row was dying, and yet the new Row was still a dream. But the dreamers did come. In 1964, the irrepressible Dick O'Kane and his Warehouse Restaurant in the old brick Booth Reduction plant, "the joint that kept Cannery Row famous," was soon followed by others. In 1968, the lead was taken by the Sardine Factory of Ted Balestreri and Bert Cutino, in the old Portuguese Aurora Hall, forming the Cannery Row Company. As if propelled by restaurants, the new Row began the slow rise of the Phoenix, rising from its own ashes, born on new wings of a quaint, funky, historical tourism looking for John Steinbeck, "Doc," and Mack and the boys. Now you know them, and you can find them and their haunts if you search carefully under the lively commercial veneer of the modern Cannery Row. It is, according to this historian, "America's Most Famous Street."

Monterey Bay

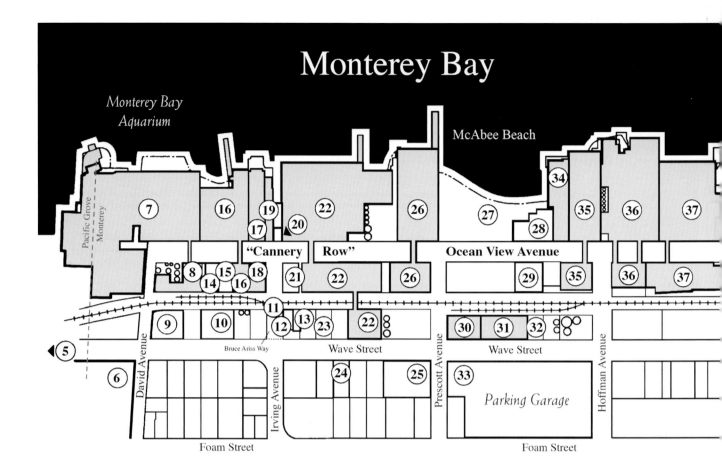

Monterey Bay Aquarium

McAbee Beach

"Cannery" "Row"

Ocean View Avenue

Bruce Ariss Way

Wave Street

David Avenue

Irving Avenue

Prescott Avenue

Hoffman Avenue

Wave Street

Parking Garage

Foam Street

Foam Street

Pacific Grove

Monterey

Point Ohlones, "China Point"
(Not to scale above)

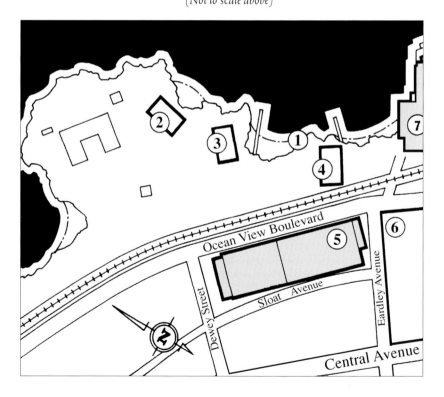

Ocean View Boulevard

Dewey Street

Sloat Avenue

Eardley Avenue

Central Avenue

Historic
CANNERY ROW

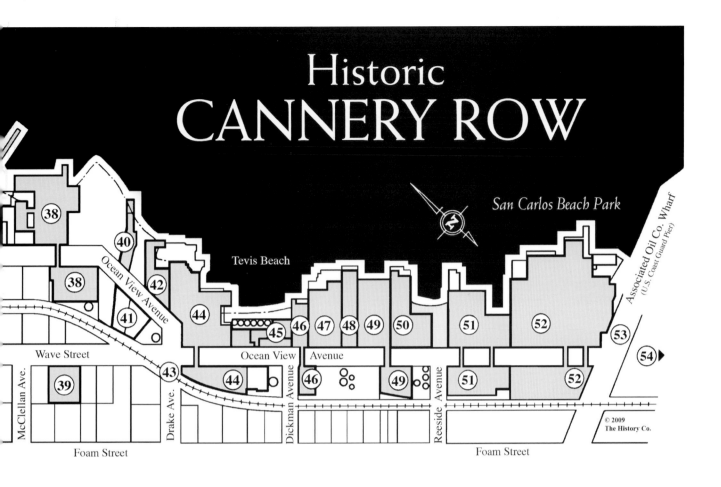

San Carlos Beach Park

Tevis Beach

Associated Oil Co. Wharf
(U.S. Coast Guard Pier)

Wave Street

Ocean View Avenue

McClellan Ave.

Drake Ave.

Dickman Avenue

Reeside Avenue

Ocean View Avenue

Foam Street

Foam Street

© 2009
The History Co.

Booth cannery and wharf
and Fisherman's Wharf

Ted McKay [83-006-005]

THE HISTORY COMPANY
www.TheHistoryCompany.com

Old Row Map Index

www.TheHistoryCompany.com

1. CHINATOWN. 1853-1906. Burned May 6, 1906. Chinese lease McAbee Beach and establish another, smaller Chinatown, 1907-1924. Cannery expansion removes them.

2. HOPKINS MARINE STATION. Originally Stanford's Hopkins Seaside Laboratory, located at Lovers Point, Pacific Grove. Moved to China Point in 1917.

3. MONTEREY BOAT WORKS. Established by Pearson and Cochran in 1915. Bought out by Gus Smith circa 1919. Bought by Siino Boat Works in 1937.

4. SIINO BOAT WORKS, 1928-1937. Consolidated with Monterey Boat Works in 1937. Built lampara boats and, later, the cannery hoppers for purse seiners.

5. AMERICAN CAN COMPANY. 1927. Its first manager, Donald E. McDonald, claimed its first year production would be 65,000,000 cans. Closed in 1954.

6. T. A. WORK LUMBERYARD. Established in the early years of cannery construction by local investor.

7. HOVDEN FOOD PRODUCTS CORP. 1916-1973. Norwegian-born canning innovator Knut Hovden, left pioneer packer, Frank Booth, to open his own cannery on Ocean View Avenue. Burns August 11, 1921 and was rebuilt. Reduction plant blaze October 5, 1924 lasts two days. "The King of Cannery Row" retired in 1951. Its historic concrete warehouse welcomes visitors to the Monterey Bay Aquarium.

8. HOVDEN FISH MEAL WAREHOUSE. Burned in 197? Now administration offices of the Monterey Bay Aquarium.

9. McFADDEN'S, (also the John Baker House of the "King of Wave Street") now known as the "OLD COAST HOUSE." A canning era home and boarding house.

10. FISH MEAL BARN above the tracks, behind the WING CHONG MARKET—the model for John Steinbeck's "Palace Flophouse" in Cannery Row.

11. "CHICKEN WALK" in Cannery Row. Cleated planks (as in a chicken coup) up the embankment from the tracks to the unfinished Irving Avenue. Now "Bruce Ariss Way."

12. "PALACE FLOPHOUSE" in its actual location as a triplex for single cannery workers (though described as the fish meal barn in #9) Cannery Row, Chapters 1 and 7. It shared a small lot with the JOSS HOUSE (3rd location).

13. CHINESE JOSS HOUSE. Burned on this site in March of 1942, damaging the adjacent "Palace Flophouse."

14. LA IDA CAFE. 1929. One of the Row's "houses of ill repute." Cannery Row. Chapter 7.

15. WING CHONG MARKET. Won Yee and eleven Chinese Investors open a grocery and dry-goods store, September 1918. Cannery Row, Chapter 1.

16. The Japanese-owned GREAT WESTERN SARDINE CO. (1917) becomes SEA PRIDE PACKING CO. in 1925. Sells to Stewart and Irving in 1929, becoming ATLANTIC COAST FISHERIES in December 1945. Cannery burns in 1980.

17. MONTEREY FISH PRODUCTS. Established in 1915 by fish meal "reduction" pioneer, Max M. Schaefer.

18. "VACANT LOT" and BLACK CYPRESS of Cannery Row. Introduction and Chapter 1. Location of MALLOY'S BOILER, Chapter 8. Often mistaken for the vacant end of Irving Street.

19. DEL VISTA PACKING CO. 1946. A late entry into the reduction business, owned by the Yee family.

20. PACIFIC BIOLOGICAL LABORATORIES. 1929. Edward F. Ricketts moved his biological supply business from Pacific Grove. Appears as "Western Biological Laboratory" in Cannery Row, Chapters 5, 10, 20, 21 and 30. A private men's club since 1958. Now owned and preserved by the City of Monterey: one of few sites on the National Register of Historic Places in the entire Cannery Row district.

21. FLORA WOOD'S LONE STAR CAFE. 1923-1941. The "Bear Flag Restaurant" of "Dora Flood"— the Row's most notorious bordello and its most magnanimous madam—Chapters 3 and 16 of Cannery Row. Flora dies in poverty in an apartment on Alvarado street on August 1, 1948.

22. BAYSIDE FISH AND FLOUR CO. 1916. Became Cypress Canning Company, September, 1927. Became DEL MAR CANNING CO. on January 26, 1928. A major fire November 25, 1936, also destroys Ed Ricketts' Lab. Both are rebuilt. Burns as WEST GATE-SUN HARBOR on December 8, 1951.

23. Home of QUOCK MUI, "Spanish Mary," Chinese leader born at Point Lobos, 1859; multi-lingual cannery worker; and advocate for the Chinese integration into Monterey.

24. MOW WO'S. A Chinese grocery and hardware store established in the early 1920s.

25. AURORA HALL. An early 1920s YMCA, Spanish Hall, boxing ring and cannery worker's cafeteria. Became the flagship restaurant of Cannery Row, the Sardine Factory, 1968.

26. MONTEREY CANNING CO. 1918. Constructed on the site of the Chinese "Monterey Fish Canning Co." (1910-1916) by Scotsmen George Harper, and A. M. Allan (partner with Gennosuke Kodani in the Point Lobos abalone cannery). Burned in 1978; its warehouse remains original.

27. McABEE BEACH. Early Portuguese shore-whaling station from the 1860s, named for the Scot whose beach cottages and boat rental replaced whaling from this beach near the turn of the century. Many Chinese relocated to this smaller site, leased to them by San Franciscan, John McAbee, after the fire at China Point in 1906.

28. OCEAN VIEW HOTEL. 1927-1983. Built and owned by Mr. and Mrs. Maen Chang Wu on part of the McABEE BEACH CHINATOWN site (1907-1924). The post-sardine 1950s recovery began at Neil DeVaughn's restaurant in it.

29. MARINA APARTMENTS. 1929. An annex to the Ocean View Hotel built by the Wu's. It became an "institution of commercialized love."

30. F. E. BOOTH REDUCTION PLANT. Construction begins October 2, 1917 as Booth's late entry into large-scale fish meal and fertilizer production. It could not be located with his cannery in the harbor.

31. EDGEWATER PACKING CO. Added to the World War I era F. E. Booth brick reduction plant, circa 1940.

32. The home of YEE SING JUNG, 638 Wave Street. The home of Yee Sing Jung (fourth son of Quock Mui, #23) built in the late 1920s as part of the Row's "Third Chinatown" in the streets above Ocean View Avenue as the McAbee Beach settlement was demolished and the Ocean View Hotel was constructed on its site.

33. UNION SUPPLY COMPANY. Lumber mill and yard owned by Henry Hansen. Now a municipal parking lot.

34. SEA BEACH PACKING CO. Ground-breaking in September, 1945. Bums in 1953.

35. CUSTOM HOUSE PACKING CORP. 1929-1952. Closes in November 1952. Burns in October 1953.

36. CARMEL CANNING CO. 1918-1962. Ben Senderman retires, selling his new cannery to local investors. It burns in 1967.

37. MONTEREY FISHING AND CANNING CO. 1902. Harry Malpas and Otosaburo Noda build the first cannery on the New Monterey coastline. It becomes PACIFIC FISH CO. in August, 1908—the first major canning operation on what was to become Cannery Row. It was bought by CALIFORNIA PACKING CORP. on March 1, 1926. Closes in April, 1962. Burns in 1967 and 1973.

38. SAN XAVIER CANNING CO. 1917. Frank Raiter's "San X" cannery burns in 1967. Its reduction plant remains.

39. CARMEL CANNING COMPANY WAREHOUSE. A Wave Street satellite warehouse on the National Register of Historic Places.

40. WESTERN SARDINE CO. Construction begins on this reduction plant in December, 1945.

41. Early addresses of Ben Senderman and the Hovden's. Constructed as support houses for the TEVIS ESTATE near the turn of the century. An R.K.O. film, "Clash By Night," shot in 1951 and premiered in 1952, starred Barbara Stanwyck and Marilyn Monroe. Became home and offices of the "Mayor of Cannery Row," New Row era businessman, Frank Crispo.

42. THE FERRANTE CO. Built by Sal Ferrante, son- in-law of Pietro Ferrante, in a furious wartime cannery expansion,1945.

43. Cannery Row Foundation ED RICKETTS MEMORIAL at the site of his collision with the evening Del Monte Express, May 8, 1948. Born May 14, 1897; he dies May 11,1948. John Steinbeck details the tragedy as part of "About Ed Ricketts," the preface to The Log From the Sea of Cortez. 1951.

44. OXNARD CANNING CO. Sal Ferrante builds this huge cannery in five war-time months, opening in October, 1942.

40-49. TEVIS-MURRAY ESTATE. 1901-1944. Hugh Tevis died on his honeymoon; the palatial estate built for his bride sold to James A. Murray in 1904. The estate occupied nearly 1,000 feet of Monterey's scenic coastline (sites 40 through 49). Sold in mid 1940s to become canneries and reduction plants.

45. WESTERN FISH PROCESSORS. July 1943. A "stick-water" (waste water) treatment plant that reduced liquid canning waste into concentrated by-products—helping account for Monterey's horrendous reduction process odor.

46. AENEAS SARDINE PACKING CO. 1945. Its cannery-to-warehouse "cross-over" is one of only two originals left on the Row. Like many late entries to the industry, it was to be the victim of poor timing.

47. CENTRAL PACKING CO. A WWII reduction plant constructed on the Tevis Estate site.

48. RONADA FISHERIES and MAGNOLIA PACKING CO. Late 1940s entries into the reduction process.

49. ENTERPRISE PACKERS. The warehouse building remains of this cannery, constructed in 1945 during World War II demand and just proceeding the disappearance of the sardines.

50. CALIFORNIA FISHERIES CO. 1916. A Japanese export firm destroyed by the oil tank fire of September, 1924. Sal Ventimiglia builds CALIFORNIA FROZEN FISH CO. on the vacant site in 1945.

51. E. B. GROSS CANNING CO. 1919-1943. Funston-Gross Packing destroyed by the 1924 oil tank fire and rebuilt. Ed Gross sells in 1943 to PENINSULA PACKING CO.

52. SAN CARLOS CANNING CO. 1927. Angelo Lucido headed this major cannery that was owned by boat owners and fishermen. It burns on Thanksgiving, 1956.

53. COALINGA OIL AND TRANSPORTATION PIER. 1904. Also known as the Associated Oil Company Pier, this 650-foot pier was destroyed by the oil fire of 1924 at storage tanks for the terminus of a pipeline from Coalinga. Monterey's BREAKWATER began construction on its pilings. 1934.

54. F. E. BOOTH CO. 1903-1941. In 1903, Booth buys out his competitor H. R. Bobbin's rudimentary plant and expands it into the first major canning operation of Monterey's sardine era. "The Father of the Sardine-Industry" is forced out of business in 1941 by fellow cannery owners who help ensure that his municipal lease in the harbor is not renewed. He closes May 28,1941. He dies December 12, 1941. It's wharf, roughly parallel to Monterey's Fisherman's Wharf, did not survive the demise of the cannery.

55. "POP" ERNEST DOELTER'S seafood restaurant, "home of the abalone streak." Pop Ernest Doelter dies in 1934. The restaurant, run by his sons, struggles until closing in 1952.

PART TWO:
New Horizons for
Cannery Row-Monterey and
Pacific Northwest History

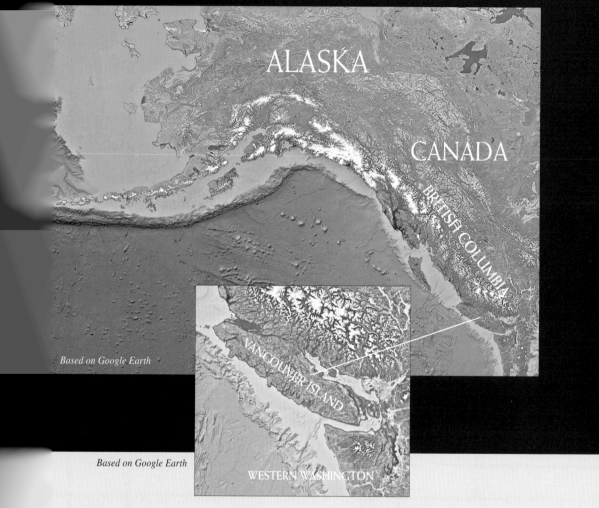

ALASKA

CANADA

BRITISH COLUMBIA

Based on Google Earth

VANCOUVER ISLAND

Based on Google Earth

WESTERN WASHINGTON

The purpose of this special section is to identify and connect significant historical, maritime, literary, and ecological legacies that Cannery Row and Monterey share with the greater maritime Pacific Northwest. This endeavor is a work in progress to identify, introduce, connect and celebrate these separate but related realms in order to more fully appreciate their correlation in a rich new horizon, a new vision, of Monterey and Pacific Northwest history. This is an effort to bring emerging awareness, consciousness and enjoyment of what we share. An inspiration sprang from the image by Jack Calvin that sparked an urgent need to research, connect, illuminate, and share what we have yet to fully appreciate.

Ed Ricketts at Point Wilson lighthouse at Port Townsend, Washington, July 25, 1930. Jack Calvin. [2006-024-0001]

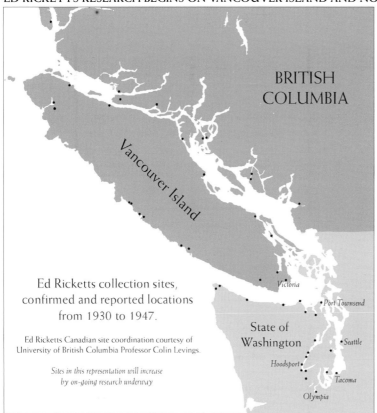

Ed Ricketts collection sites,
confirmed and reported locations
from 1930 to 1947.

Ed Ricketts Canadian site coordination courtesy of
University of British Columbia Professor Colin Levings.

*Sites in this representation will increase
by on-going research underway*

Ed Ricketts in Army hat and beard with a net helper across this tide pool.   [88-010-0001]

*Ed Ricketts in 1935 shown with his 1930 Packard 7-40 limousine in Carmel Valley, California.
He replaced it in early 1937 with a Ford V-8 coupe.*   Ed Ricketts, Jr. [2005-025-0001]

In the summer of 1930, Ed Ricketts was drawn to travel north to the Pacific Northwest's vast, changing topographical inventory of open ocean, shorelines, bluffs, sounds, and estuaries for study and collection of marine biological species. Motivation was part surveillance and part collection for his Pacific Biological Laboratories. Ed was constantly developing his contacts, correspond and sending samples literally all over the county. But above all else, he was driven by his focus on his approach to the organization and interconnection of organisms we now know as ecology. Ed's struggling biological supply business, with help from John Steinbeck, funded his passion for pressing on. He spent most of the decade of the 1930s impatiently waiting for Stanford University Press to finally publish his revolutionary ecological approach to aggregations of life we now know today as Ecology: "Between Pacific Tides."

Jack Calvin, though not a marine scientist was a Stanford University graduate, a professional writer and teacher. Jack was host to a Bohemian-like literary group that gathered at Sasha Calvin's art studio-cottage [Page 92] next to the main Calvin house in Carmel Woods. It is there that Ed Ricketts and John and Carol Steinbeck, Ritchie and Tal Lovejoy, Toby Street, and A. Grove Day, and others became friends and met regularly at the Calvin's. Jack's friendship with Ed easily led to helping Ed with collections and then his sometime tortured prose. But he was more than Ed's editor; he became partner in the effort to publish a handbook on the intertidal zones of the West Coast. The eventual result "Between Pacific Tides" was intended for use by lay people and the field of marine biologists.

Ed evolved as leader of the group after Jack and Sasha Calvin moved to Sitka and the group needed a new meeting place. Ed's new Lab on Cannery Row had just been completed and was a natural Great Depression gathering place. Ed also had a car, a phone, a washing machine and an Encyclopedia Britannica. None of his friends had any of those extravagances but enjoyed his thoroughly.

One thing was certain. You couldn't find Ed at home in the Lab on Cannery Row in spring or summer during the 1930s. He was on a shoreline between Juneau and Ensenada. His great unfinished endeavor remained the Pacific Northwest which would complete the "Trilogy" of his work to observe, study, collect, and publish his ecological inter-tidal marine biological survey of the entire coast of North America—alone! Fate had other plans for Ed Ricketts.

May 1948, Ed anticipated his return to the Queen Charlotte Islands (now Haida Gwai), this time with John Steinbeck—from were they were to embark on another Sea of Cortez-like Expedition. The trip would extend up the British Columbia coast to Alaska and out to the Bering Sea and Aleutian Islands—with a book based on the trip with another two-part design with a detailed scientific section mated, as with the "Sea of Cortez," with a narrative of the inter-tidal coastline and details of the trip by John Steinbeck. But everything suddenly changed.

The evening Del Monte Express train through Cannery Row struck Ed's immobilized 1936 Buick, carrying the battered car several hundred feet before it could be stopped. Ed was crushed between the driver's side door and the door post, having taken too long to get out of the car. [Page 109]

Calvins, Ricketts, and Campbell group with the Calvin's "Nakwasina" Willits canoe, which Jack and Shasa rowed from Tacoma to Sitka on their honeymoon. [99-026-006]

Ed Ricketts experienced the vast and diversified collection realm of the Pacific Northwest on his 1930 trip with Jack Calvin to Northwest Washington and Vancouver Island. The advances achieved and the rich collection opportunities in the Pacific Northwest made major contributions to forming his ecological vision.

In July of 1930 his foray into upper Vancouver Island in British Columbia reached at least as far as Comox. We also know from his surviving collecting records that he reconnoitered ocean-ward on the northern rim of the State of Washington, along the banks and beaches of the Strait of Juan de Fuca. He, of course, collected at Port Townsend as seen in the iconic photo of Jack Calvin's of Ed in the bull kelp at the Point Wilson lighthouse. Farther south he's known to have inspected the tidal shore life at Puget Sound's Wollochet Bay, near Gig Harbor.

Road access at this point to many collection sites did not represent a serious obstacle, but many more lay beyond reach by road and by foot. Ed's introduction to the only real solution was made possible by Jack Calvin. In early 1932, a charter for a scientific voyage from Puget Sound to Calvin's realm in Alaska presented an incredible opportunity that would solidify Ed's relationship to the entire Pacific Northwest. The ocean and bay shorelines, the streams and river deltas, marshes and mud flats of the north created a permanent scientific bond with Ed that would last the rest of his life.

Ed Ricketts busy with processing his specimens after a day of collecting. [99-026-005]

Jack Calvin was elated to take the Pacific Biological Laboratories charter of the Grampus from Tacoma to Juneau. His real expertise as a boat man was matched with his intimate familiarity with the course of the journey. The Willits Brothers "Nakwasina" canoe of his honeymoon was lashed to the top of the Grampus. The crew would be composed of Jack and Sasha Calvin, Ed Ricketts and Joseph Campbell for the 10-week cruise up Puget Sound, into the Salish Sea, through the strait of Georgia between the B.C. mainland and Vancouver Island, across Queen Charlotte Sound (Haida Gwaii) to the southern tip of Alaska, and up to Sitka and then Juneau. Once at Juneau the group enlarged to include Xenia Kashaverov, Tal and Sasha's younger sister, their father–the Orthodox Priest of Juneau– and other of their friends.

The experience at Sitka impressed Ed immensely as he declared Sitka Sound the most incredible and abundant collection site anywhere. During the course of the voyage Ed Ricketts and Joseph Campbell spent much time in discussions of science, nature, culture, mysticism, philosophy, and life. Eric Enno Tamm best makes the case of how Ed Ricketts not only influenced John Steinbeck as a writer, but how he also impacted the keen mind of Joseph Campbell at a time he was searching for direction in his own life. Campbell credits his short two months next door to Ricketts in Pacific Grove and his ten weeks with him on the Grampus for the direction that has him in turn crediting Ricketts as his later transcendent "Hero With a Thousand Faces."

Sitka, in June of 1932 . The Grampus would soon be present. [2015-033-0001]

The Gateway Inn and Cabins at Hoodsport, shown here on the banks of the Hood Canal, was one of over forty inns and summer guest cabins on the Hood Canal by the 1930s. Ed Ricketts' daughter, Nancy, recalls their cabin there (believed to be the far left on the shoreline) as a nearly annual family base of operations for her father's research and collecting from Hoodsport to Eldon, Union, Twanoh, and Tanhuya, with nearer to Belfair an extraordinary low-oxygen aquatic study area.   [2018-034-003]

The earlier Dickinsen's Gateway Hotel at Hoodsport was originally the home of prominent settler and lumber Capt. Geroge Robbins. It became the Gateway Inn and Cabins. With railroad development failing and improved road access eventually completed only in the early 1930s, its accomodations life ended well before the site became a state salmon hatchery in 1953.   *[Mason County Historical Society photo]*

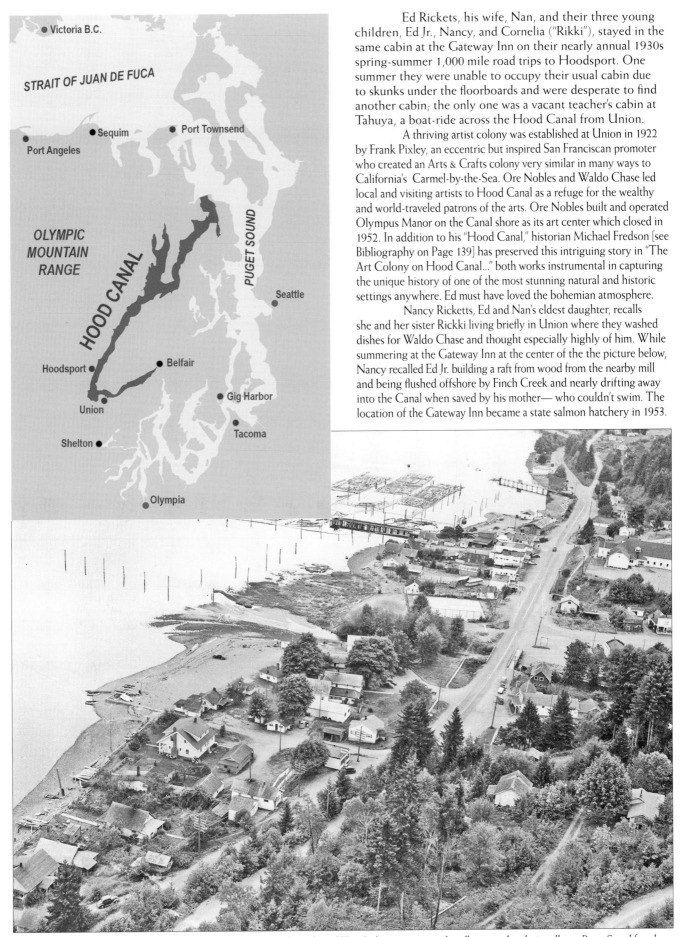

Ed Rickets, his wife, Nan, and their three young children, Ed Jr., Nancy, and Cornelia ("Rikki"), stayed in the same cabin at the Gateway Inn on their nearly annual 1930s spring-summer 1,000 mile road trips to Hoodsport. One summer they were unable to occupy their usual cabin due to skunks under the floorboards and were desperate to find another cabin; the only one was a vacant teacher's cabin at Tahuya, a boat-ride across the Hood Canal from Union.

A thriving artist colony was established at Union in 1922 by Frank Pixley, an eccentric but inspired San Franciscan promoter who created an Arts & Crafts colony very similar in many ways to California's Carmel-by-the-Sea. Ore Nobles and Waldo Chase led local and visiting artists to Hood Canal as a refuge for the wealthy and world-traveled patrons of the arts. Ore Nobles built and operated Olympus Manor on the Canal shore as its art center which closed in 1952. In addition to his "Hood Canal," historian Michael Fredson [see Bibliography on Page 139] has preserved this intriguing story in "The Art Colony on Hood Canal..." both works instrumental in capturing the unique history of one of the most stunning natural and historic settings anywhere. Ed must have loved the bohemian atmosphere.

Nancy Ricketts, Ed and Nan's eldest daughter, recalls she and her sister Rikki living briefly in Union where they washed dishes for Waldo Chase and thought especially highly of him. While summering at the Gateway Inn at the center of the the picture below, Nancy recalled Ed Jr. building a raft from wood from the nearby mill and being flushed offshore by Finch Creek and nearly drifting away into the Canal when saved by his mother— who couldn't swim. The location of the Gateway Inn became a state salmon hatchery in 1953.

In the summer of 1942, prior to Ed's induction into Army for the second time, he and Toni Jackson spent six weeks collecting and exploring all over Puget Sound from here. It is possible that Ed's 1937 model Ford V-8 coupe, which replaced his Packard limo, is at the far bottom left of this exceptional aerial photo. [2018-034-0002]

Ed and Tony at Kildonan Cannery, Vancouver Island, B.C. in 1946 doing research for the "Outer Shores."   *Ed Ricketts Jr. [98-083-0016]*

Without a Guggenheim grant, institutional backing, or sponsorship of any kind–other than occasional financial help from John Steinbeck–Ed Ricketts revolutionized marine biology and introduced ecology while doing it. And he did it with much of the maritime Pacific Northwest's shorelines under his feet. Ed used his intermittent biological supply house income to fuel his self-funded passion to complete the most comprehensive inter-tidal marine biological survey and study of the West Coast of North America ever undertaken.

All of Ed Ricketts' 1,000 mile forays from Monterey to the marine biological study and collection sites of northern shores of Washington State and especially those all over British Columbia's Vancouver Island, the Strait of Georgia, and the "inland passage" toward the Queen Charlotte Islands (Haida Gwaii) and Alaska were at his own Expense. This feat in itself is quite astonishing in that the Great Depression's impact on financial matters of every description held sway through the 1930s. The rather extreme extent of his travels from Monterey to his southern ventures as far as upper Baja below Ensenada, and northward from Monterey to the far side of British Columbia's Vancouver Island is extraordinary. But it didn't end there.

Ed's devotion to the saltwater shorelines of all kinds to be found from Washington to Alaska contributed in major measure to a "toto" view and strategic plan for an integrated understanding of the inter-relatedness of marine species from Baja to the Aleutian Islands.

The month after Ed's death in May 1948, was to be another "Sea of Cortez" style expedition with Steinbeck, this one to the great Pacific Northwest to complete Ed 's "Trilogy": the complete inter-tidal marine biological survey of the west coast's northern hemisphere shorelines from the Sea of Cortez to the Aleutian Islands. Ed's sudden departure stunned not only John Steinbeck deeply, but everyone who knew Ed, even the one's who knew him as "Doc" Ricketts.

If you wish to dive deeper into the information that the text and images in this book has been constructed to present, I recommend a reading, or re-reading, of "**Cannery Row**" by John Steinbeck. It is our hope that what you have now read and observed in this book should confirm the extraordinary relationship between Ed Ricketts and John Steinbeck in what we believe is the greatest symbiosis of science and literature in the American experience, and far beyond.

With John Steinbeck's iconic basis of Cannery Row literature in mind, stepping into the non-fiction world of a choice short-list of the works that demonstrate the blend of histories ahead begins with Kevin Bailey and his "**The Western Flyer, Steinbeck's boat, The Sea of Cortez, and the Saga of the Western Flyer**"; the "**Log From the Sea of Cortez**" by John Steinbeck (1951) derived from "**Sea of Cortez**" by Steinbeck and Ricketts (1940); "**Beyond the Outer Shores**" by Eric Enno Tamm; and the *tour de force* I've been waiting for by my incredible colleagues–Drexel University's Dr. Richard Astro and Hopkins Marine Station Miller Librarian Donald Kohrs and their "**A Tidal Odyssey, Ed Ricketts and the Making of Between Pacific Tides.**"

These are core books and are all recommended as fascinating and essential to the fullest appreciation of the people, places, time, and consequence to the legacies shared between Monterey-Cannery Row and the greater maritime Pacific Northwest. More of this background awaits in the *Bibliography on page 139.*

That history is still being written. With the appreciation of the Croatian boat builders of Puget Sound providing Monterey's Sicilians, another immigrant nationality to the Pacific Coast, with the ability of making Monterey a world-famous fishery capable of feeding our world's free nations through two world wars.

The Pacific Northwestern Croatian and Californian Sicilian connections now deserve some special detail as we now begin to enter the inter-personal relationships that boat building and fishing wrought.

The Western Flyer after the May 4, 1937 launch at the Western Boat Building Company of Martin A. Petrich   *[Petrich Family Collection]*

Advanced northwestern-built purse-seiners began to show up in southern California ports in the early 1920s. Within a few seasons of their arrival in Monterey in the 1926-1927 sardine season the ascendancy of the purse-seine craft for sardines and salmon was also responsible for a decades later corresponding appearance of some Monterey boats to Puget Sound, to the Salish Sea, to the Gulf of Alaska, and the Aleutians: this was an amazing tide pool...and still is.

The predominantly Croatian boat-building industry around Tacoma in south Puget Sound ascended to the pinnacle of our country's wooden boat building era. As previously stated, it made it possible for Monterey's dominantly Sicilian fleet to make Monterey the "Sardine Capital of the World" during World War II.

Most of the men and boats are gone but have left a legacy that helps bind a maritime heritage still alive on the entire west coast of the North American coastline. That heritage is most alive and celebrated in the maritime Pacific Northwest. The new element is the presence of the most famous fishing boat in the world, the Western Flyer—renamed the Gemini in 1970—which brings a new level of stimulation to the restorations in-progress and preservation of other historic boats in the maritime Pacific Northwest and elsewhere.

Of all the vessels built the Pacific Northwest, none is more famous that the Western Flyer, forever earning Tacoma's pride and celebration as the "The Birthplace of the Western Flyer."

However, it must be recognized that it is not only the sardine and salmon fisheries that are sole historical beneficiaries of the exceptional, if often devastating efficiency of the Pacific Northwest's exceedingly successful fishing vessels. The case of the Monterey fleet's efficiency beyond the bounds of reasonable and responsible catches by its northern-built boats, contributed significantly to the loss of its sardine fishery, once considered inexhaustible. That lesson was to be lost on the magnificent fisheries of the Pacific Northwest.

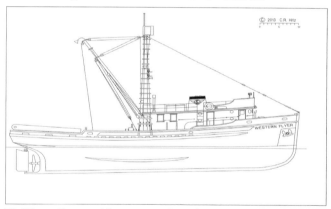

The Western Flyer rigged for seining Pacific Northwest waters. [Bob Hitz graphic]

After the Western Flyer's life of operating from the Port of Monterey from 1938 to 1948 ended with the onset of the crash of the "inexhaustible supply of Monterey sardines"–and with little real prospect of its immediate recovery–there was nothing left but to return the Western Flyer to Puget Sound. Tony Berry would not return with it; instead he stayed on at Monterey for the rest of his life as a respected member of the community while suffering a non-stop bane of reporters and people (too many writers) wanting to know about Steinbeck, Ed Ricketts, the Western Flyer, and the Sea of Cortez.

The return of the Western Flyer to northwestern waters saw the end to her purse-seining era and her re-rigged for trawling a succession of Pacific Northwest fisheries under the same strain as what she had experienced in Monterey. All of this is presented by University of Washington fisheries scientist, Kevin Bailey, in his "The Western Flyer: Steinbeck's Boat, The Sea of Cortez, and The Saga of Pacific Fisheries." *Recommended in the Bibliography. Page 139.*

Tony Berry and his father Frank were partners in the building of the Western Flyer with owner of the Western Boat Building Company, Martin A. Petrich. Tony became Western Flyer's skipper.   [Petrich Family Collection]

Monterey Peninsula Herald

MONTEREY, CALIFORNIA, TUESDAY, MARCH 20, 1984

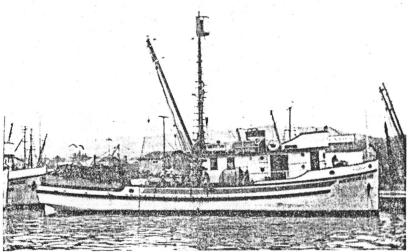

THE WESTERN FLYER IN MONTEREY HARBOR DURING THE EARLY '40s
... photo is from the collection of the Allen Knight Maritime Museum

Boat Steinbeck Used Located, May Come Back to Monterey

The Western Flyer hunched into the great waves toward Cedros Island, the wind blew off the tops of the whitecaps, and the big guy wire, from bow to mast, took up its vibration like the low pipe on a tremendous organ. It sang its deep note into the wind.
— from "The Log From the Sea of Cortez," by John Steinbeck

In 1940, John Steinbeck chartered a Monterey purse seiner, the Western Flyer, to conduct a marine biological expedition into Baja California with his friend and mentor, "Doc" Ed Ricketts.

The voyage resulted not only in the collection of more than 1,000 species of marine life, but also in the publication of "The Log From the Sea of Cortez," which Steinbeck wrote from Ricketts' journals.

Now the Western Flyer has been located, according to Michael Hemp, executive director of the Cannery Row Foundation. At a meeting last Thursday the foundation's board of directors endorsed the concept of attempting to buy the boat and bring it back to Monterey.

Hemp said the 76-foot boat, which was built in Tacoma, Wash., in 1937, is still in service "on this coast, in this country" and does not require a major restoration.

"It's not a rehabilitation project and it's not a basket case," he said.

The foundation does not want to disclose the present whereabouts of the boat until negotiations for an option to purchase it have been concluded, for fear of driving up the price, Hemp said.

What Hemp terms a "blue-ribbon commission of individuals and organizations with mutual interests in the acquisition of this historic symbol of Monterey's past" has been formed to examine possible financing for the project, the legal aspects, and the feasibility of acquiring the boat.

Tony Berry, who was skipper for the Steinbeck-Ricketts voyage, and Horace "Sparky" Enea, who was crewman and cook, are both still living in Monterey and would be available to oversee the return of the Western Flyer and restoration of the boat to her 1940 configuration, Hemp said.

The boat would be berthed or moored in the harbor and could be visited by schools and other special interest groups. It could also serve as a meeting place for "senior members of the Monterey fishing community," Hemp said, and as a floating classroom, where demonstrations such as the setting of a purse-seine net could be performed.

Hemp said a "ballpark" figure for purchase of the boat would be about $100,000. If the option to purchase it can be acquired, the foundation will seek out individuals interested in helping to finance the project, he said.

"This is a bootstrap program, like everything else the Cannery Row Foundation has done," Hemp said.

The non-profit foundation organized The Great Cannery Row Reunion last May (another is scheduled May 18-19 of this year) and has received approval from the City of Monterey for a Cannery Row Workers Memorial Park, to be developed on city-owned property on the row

The first ever public announcement of the location of the Western Flyer and the earliest effort to recover her for return to Monterey as a world-famous working scientific and public charter.

Bob Enea   [MK Hemp Photo]

Gemini, as Bob Enea found it.   [Pat Hathaway photo 1983]

We likely owe the very existence of the Western Flyer today to Monterey's fishing industry historian Bob Enea, the nephew of not only one of the Western Flyer builder-partners and skipper, Tony Berry, but also a nephew of deck hand Horace, "Sparky" Enea on the 1940 voyage of the Western Flyer to the Sea of Cortez. Thanks to Bob's extended fishing family and others in Monterey's fishing community he had a pretty good idea where in the Pacific Northwest the Western Flyer might be found, though many people dismissed the idea that the Western Flyer still existed at all.

In late 1983, shortly after the Establishment of the non-profit Cannery Row Foundation, Bob asked me, "Hey, Mike...how would you like to get a hold of the Western Flyer?" He didn't have to inquire twice. But actually finding her and then attempting acquisition were to prove to be more than a 30 year Odyssey.

Years later, Bob finally located her by her radio call sign, WB 4404–or on the radio as "Whisky Bravo forty-four-oh-four" –a call sign which did not change when the name of the boat changed to Gemini, which occurred in the Pacific Northwest in 1970!

The fledgling Cannery Row Foundation had insufficient funding to do little more than its core purpose to capture the fading history of old Cannery Row itself before it was lost. And yet in 1984 the news of the Foundation's attempt to acquire her failed to report that Bob Enea was responsible for it all.

Bob Enea, however, was not to be denied. Becoming a board member of the National Steinbeck Center in Salinas he marshalled an acquisition plan which eventually failed only due to the Center's own financial priorities.

In 2010, Bob created the non-profit Western Flyer Project to acquire the vessel. In 2011 a businessman outbid for the Gemini, moored on a channel near Anacortes, Washington. It sank twice at its mooring and was towed to Port Townsend. It was bought in 2015 by marine geologist, John Gregg, paying a million dollars for a boat that didn't float: "It was worthless...but it was priceless." Salvation of the Western Flyer was proclaimed by John Gregg at a Symposium held by the Cannery Row Foundation at Stanford's Hopkins Marine Station, Pacific Grove. Soon thereafter restoration began at the Port Townsend Shipwright's Co-op. The Western Flyer Foundation was formed to restore and operate the Western Flyer from Home Port Monterey as a voyaging scientific classroom–from maritime Pacific Northwest to the Sea of Cortez– dedicated to inspiring youth into the marine sciences.

THE WESTERN FLYER BECOMES THE GEMINI

The Western Flyer on 1962-63 Pacific Halibut Commission surveys of trawling impacts, from Cape Spencer to Kodiak Island. (Map page 127) Colin Levings photo.

Late July, 1964: Western Flyer crabbing in the Gulf of Alaska broke down and was listing, taking on water before U.S. Coast Guard aircraft arrived with pumps. The photographer was aboard on the 1962-1963 halibut survey.   Colin Levings photo.

Gemini at Homer, Alaska. Acquired by the Fry family in 1976.   Dennis Fry photo.

Clarence Fry set immediately to converting the Gemini from trawler to crabber and replaced the original chain steering with hydraulic controls and modern navigational instruments. Two of his sons assisted with the updates needed to make her fit and competitive in far northern waters.

Gemini moored at Anacortes, Washington. She sank here in late 2012 and again in early 2013. Refloated, she was towed to Port Townsend.   Kevin Bailey photo.

Gemini at Port Townsend, 2013 .   Anne Shaffer, Coastal Watershed Institute

Dennis Fry on an earlier boat at Homer, Alaska. He kept the Gemini navigational hardware – now treasured artifacts of the Western Flyer.   Dennis Fry photo.

When Clarence Fry and his sons replaced the Gemini's chain steering and brass navigation controls with a hydraulic system, for some reason one of his sons decided to hang onto the brass flying bridge ship's wheel, it's three-part brass helm-stand, the brass articulated shift lever (forward-neutral-reverse), and both the main deck house compass and the flying bridge boxed compass.

Dennis Fry's dad, his mother, and two brothers worked the converted Monterey purse-seiner Gemini fishing for crab, halibut, and tendering salmon from newer fishing boats to the canneries in a routine shuttle system of delivery usually employing older boats.

In 1990, Dennis Fry left the family business in Homer and moved home to Hayfork, California–and for some unknown reason–was still hanging onto the brass artifacts of an anonymous old fishing boat that was really the Western Flyer. He admits to not really knowing why.

Sparky Enea, Tex Travis, Rose Berry, Tony Berry, Carol Steinbeck, John Steinbeck, and Tiny Colletto.
The missing Ed Ricketts may have taken this photo. Carol did not appear in the "The Sea of Cortez" from the trip.
[Reprinted by permission of the Martha Heasley Cox Center for Steinbeck Studies, San Jose State University]

Tex, Ed, Carol, and John in the Baby Flyer with its totally
unreliable, "Hansen Sea Cow" outboard. [Reprinted by permission
of the Martha Heasley Cox Center for Steinbeck Studies, San Jose State University]

Western Flyer voyage
to the Sea of Cortez

March 11th to
April 16th, 1940

Skipper Tony Berry on the Flying Bridge of the Western
Flyer. Steinbeck admired and trusted his skills implicitly.
[Reprinted by permission of the Martha Heasley Cox Center for Steinbeck Studies,
San Jose State University]

ABOVE: Skipper Tony Berry and John Steinbeck from the flying bridge.

LEFT: Hall "Tex" Travis, Western Flyer engineer. One of the two key men on board. From Brownfield, near Lubbock, Texas, Tex hopped a train at 18 years old and ended up in the Pacific Northwest with a talent for diesel engines, perhaps begun in Texas cotton fields before the Dust Bowl. In time, Tex's girlfriend, Louise, suggested to Tony Berry that he should date her best friend, Rose "Tootsie" Enea. Tony and Rose soon married. About a year later Tex worked engineer on Tony's Western Flyer, working Astoria, Oregon, salmon, then on to Monterey in 1938. The rest is history.

BELOW: Friendly and fun-loving, Tex took to diving off the Western Flyer on the Sea of Cortez voyage. He stayed as engineer with Tony on the boat until 1948 when the sardines crashed and be moved to North Long Beach.

[Hooley-Travis Family photos]

Tex Travis and Louise, happy newlyweds in late 1940.   [Travis Family photo]

"Tiny" Colletto and Skipper Tony Berry at the brass flying bridge wheel, now an artifact.
[Reprinted by permission of the Martha Heasley Cox Center for Steinbeck Studies, San Jose State University]

Ed Ricketts didn't believe in coincidence...only synchronicities, which was evidently at work. Rose Enea's closest girlfriend was Louise Archdeacon; they lived on the same block in Monterey. It may be that both Tex and Tony Berry both arrived in Monterey working aboard the "Sunset" in 1935. Tex and Louise became boy friend-girl friend and Louise set up a blind date with Rose and Tony. It worked: they were married before the Western Flyer began construction in Tacoma. When completed, Tony and Tex "followed the fish" to Monterey in the new Boat. Though Tony was Croatian, he was married into to the prominent Enea family and was promptly assimilated into the Sicilian dominated fleet. Another synchronicity followed in 1940 when none of the Sicilian boat owners would accept a Steinbeck charter to the Sea of Cortez.

The dilemma was resolved by Orazio Enea's intervention for his son-in-law and the Western Flyer's destiny was cast. And, as Steinbeck mentions in the narrative in the "Sea of Cortez" and it's decade later "Log from the Sea of Cortez," Tex Travis and Louise Archdeacon married after the voyage in 1940. Tony Berry and Tex Travis proved the most crucial persons aboard the Western Flyer's role in this connection of Monterey-Cannery Row to the maritime Pacific Northwest.

Tony Berry, a Petrich boat building partner and soon skipper of Western Flyer.
[Reprinted by permission of the Martha Heasley Cox Center for Steinbeck Studies, San Jose State University]

Herman "Buddy" Bendixen and daughter Laura with a Minke whale on deck of the Western Flyer at King Cove, 1966. [Bendixen Family photo]

The restored Western Flyer deck house is mated to its nearly completed hull—between storms—on January 4, 2022, at the Port Townsend Shipwrights Co-op. [Chris Chase photo]

Not very many people in Monterey knew that many of the purse-seiners in its sardine fleet, a major and unavoidable feature of Monterey's identity, were built somewhere up in the Pacific Northwest. Most boat owners and fishermen, however, were familiar with the names Scansie at Gig Harbor, Martinolich, Barbare Brothers, Western Boat Building and Martinac on Tacoma's waterfront. Monterey's Sicilians fished from Pacific Northwest Croatian-built boats, a fact lost to Monterey's public memory, but an essential inter-cultural bond.

In the early to late 1960s, the Western Flyer operated in Alaska waters, as far out as the Bering Sea and the Aleutian Islands for salmon and king crab. Fishing boats like the Western Flyer delivered to an extensive network of far northern regional canneries. The largest in the state was Peter Pan Seafoods at King Cove, on the root of the Aleutian Island chain, a remote and predominantly Aleut fishing community.

It happens that the Western Flyer had not one but two Aleut skippers: brothers Harold "Skinny" Bendixen and his younger brother Herman "Buddy" Bendixen in the 1964 through 1967 king crab seasons from King Cove [See map on Page 127]. Owner of the Western Flyer, Seattle's Dan Luketa, got very sick in 1964 and had to leave his boat and return to Ballard in Seattle. The best of his crewmen was an Aleut, who he put in charge of the boat and its crabbing. "Skinny" Bendixen took over as skipper. "Buddy" took over in 1966 and in mid-December 1966, a Minke whale got snagged in a king crab trap and drowned. The Western Flyer was not rigged to handle such a lift to the deck, but in a few hours the crew finally got it on board. Taken back to King Cove, Alaska, the local Aleut and mixed-Aleut families of the community flensed it and ate the whole whale in a matter of several days of community Christmas celebration. The Western Flyer in the Aleutians added yet again to its amazing inter-cultural lineage.

Pat Hathaway photo he took in the San Juan Islands at Lime Kiln Point Lighthouse; Gemini with Whitney-Fidalgo Seafoods ownership sign, 1983. [PH83-009-0003]

BIBLIOGRAPHY AND ADDITIONAL READING

Astro,Richard & Kohrs, Donald. A Tidal Odyssey, Ed Ricketts and the Making of Between Pacific Tides. Oregon State University Press, Corvallis, 2021.

Astro, Richard. John Steinbeck and Edward Ricketts: The Shaping of a Novelist. Minneapolis: University of Minnesota Press, 1973. Republished by Western Flyer Publishing, 2002.

Bailey, Kevin. The Western Flyer–Steinbeck's Boat, the Sea of Cortez, and the Saga of Pacific Fisheries. University of Chicago Press, 2015.

Bearden, Jean. History of Hoodsport "Gateway to the Olympics." Perry Publishing, Bremerton, Washington. 1987

Benson, Jackson J. The True Adventures of John Steinbeck, Writer. Viking Press, 1984.

Cutino, Peter T. Monterey, A View From Garlic Hill. Pacific Grove: Boxwood Press, 1995.

Elstob, Winston. Chinatown. A Legend of Old Cannery Row. Berkeley. Condor's Sky Press, 1965.

Enea, Sparky, as told to Audrey Lynch. With Steinbeck in the Sea of Cortez. Memoirs of the Steinbeck/Ricketts Expedition. Sand River Press, 1991. Reprinted in 2009 as With Steinbeck in the Sea of Cortez.

Fredson, Michael. Hood Canal, Arcadia Publishing, 2007

Fredson, Michael. The Artist Colony on Hood Canal: Pixley, Orre Nobles & Waldo Chase. Mason County Historical Society. 2011.

Gallacci, Caroline and Karabaich, Ron. Tacoma's Waterfront. Arcadia Publishing, 2006.

Hedgepeth, Joel, ed. The Outer Shores. (Volume 1 of 2 volumes). Eureka. Mad River Press, 1978.

Kohrs, Don. Edward F. Ricketts Collecting Trips Along the Pacific Coast. Stanford University-Hopkins Marine Station, Paper.

Larsen, Stephen and Robin. A Fire in the Mind, The Life of Joseph Campbell. Doubleday, 1991.

Larsh, Ed B. Doc's Lab: Myths & Legends of Cannery Row. Monterey: PBL Press, 1995.

Levings, Colin. Edward Flanders Ricketts and the marine ecology of the inner coast habitats of British Columbia, Canada. Archives of Natural History 47.1 (2020): 115–123 Edinburgh University Press.

Lundy, A. L. "Scrap." The California Abalone Industry, A Pictorial History. Best Publishing Company, 1997.

Lundy, A. L. "Scrap." Real Life on Cannery Row. People, Places and Events that Inspired John Steinbeck. Angel City Press, 2008.

Lydon, Sandy. Chinese Gold: The Chinese in the Monterey Bay Region. Capitola Book Company, 1985.

Lydon, Sandy. The Japanese in the Monterey Bay Region. A Brief History. Capitola Book Company, 1997.

Lynch, Audrey. With Steinbeck in the Sea of Cortez, by Sparky Enea as told to Audrey Lynch. Sand River Press, 1991. With Steinbeck in the Sea of Cortez. Xlibris, 2009.

Mangelsdorf, Tom. A History of Steinbeck's Cannery Row. Santa Cruz: Western Tanager Press, 1990.

McGlynn, Betty Hoag. "Casa de Las Olas" (House of the Waves; the Tevis Murray Estate). Noticias del Puerto de Monterey (Quarterly bulletin of the Monterey History and Art Association).

Reinstedt, Randy. Where Have All the Sardines Gone? Carmel: Ghost Town Publications, 1978.

Ricketts, Anna. Recollections. 1984.

Ricketts, Edward F. Between Pacific Tides. Stanford University Press. Fifth Edition, 1985.

Rodger, Katharine A. Renaissance Man of Cannery Row The Life and Letters of Edward F. Ricketts. University of Alabama Press, 2002.

Rodger, Katharine A. Breaking Through, Essays, Journals and Travelogues of Edward F. Ricketts. University of Californai Press, 2006.

Sauder, William. Mad at the World: A Life of John Steinbeck. W. W. Norton & Company, October 2020.

Shillinglaw, Susan. Carol and John Steinbeck, Portrait of a Marriage. University of Nevada Press, 2013.

Steinbeck, John. Cannery Row. Introduction by Professor Susan Shillinglaw. Penguin Edition, 1994.

Straley, Janice, ed. Ed Ricketts from Cannery Row to Sitka, Alaska. Shorefast Editions. Juneau, Alaska. 2015.

Tamm, Eric Enno. Beyond The Outer Shores. Four Walls Eight Windows Press, 2004.

Thomas, Tim and Copeland, Dennis. Monterey's Waterfront. Arcadia Publishing, 2006.

Weber, Tom. Cannery Row, A Time to Remember. Orenda/Unity Press. 1983.

Yamada, David T. The Japanese of the Monterey Peninsula, Their History & Legacy. Monterey Peninsula JACL, 1995.

INDEX

"The Row"

A street with every right
to be dead...
and odds that it should be
were it not for the
Steinbeck in all of it.
An incomplete demise
of a way of life and another time
perhaps better truly dead
than irreverenced...

— Michael Kenneth Hemp

A broadside of 1000 prints, 1980